The Get-Outside Guide to Winter Activities

Andrew Foran

Kevin Redmond

TA Loeffler

HUMAN KINETICS

Library of Congress Cataloging-in-Publication Data

Names: Foran, Andrew, author. | Redmond, Kevin, author. | Loeffler, T. A.,
      1965- author.
Title: The get-outside guide to winter activities / Andrew Foran, Kevin
      Redmond, TA Loeffler.
Description: Champaign, IL : Human Kinetics, [2016] | Includes index.
Identifiers: LCCN 2016029849| ISBN 9781492523970 (print) | ISBN 9781492546559
      (e-book)
Subjects: LCSH: Recreation leaders--Training of--Handbooks, manuals, etc. |
      Winter sports.
Classification: LCC GV181.35 .F677 2016 | DDC 796.9--dc23 LC record available at
      https://lccn.loc.gov/2016029849

ISBN: 978-1-4925-2397-0 (print)

The web addresses cited in this text were current as of July 2016, unless otherwise noted.

Acquisitions Editor: Diana Vincer; **Developmental Editor:** Jacqueline Eaton Blakley; **Managing Editors:** Anne E. Mrozek, Karla Walsh, Amy Stahl; **Copyeditor:** Patsy Fortney; **Indexer:** Nan Badgett; **Permissions Manager:** Dalene Reeder; **Graphic Designer:** Whitney Milburn; **Cover Designer:** Keith Blomberg; **Photograph (cover):** naumoid/iStock/Getty Images; **Photographs (interior):** © Human Kinetics, unless otherwise noted; **Photo Asset Manager:** Laura Fitch; **Photo Production Manager:** Jason Allen; **Senior Art Manager:** Kelly Hendren; **Printer:** Versa Press

Printed in the United States of America   10 9 8 7 6 5 4 3 2 1

The paper in this book is certified under a sustainable forestry program.

Human Kinetics
Website: www.HumanKinetics.com

United States: Human Kinetics
P.O. Box 5076
Champaign, IL 61825-5076
800-747-4457
e-mail: info@hkusa.com

Canada: Human Kinetics
475 Devonshire Road Unit 100
Windsor, ON N8Y 2L5
800-465-7301 (in Canada only)
e-mail: info@hkcanada.com

Europe: Human Kinetics
107 Bradford Road
Stanningley
Leeds LS28 6AT, United Kingdom
+44 (0) 113 255 5665
e-mail: hk@hkeurope.com

Australia: Human Kinetics
57A Price Avenue
Lower Mitcham, South Australia 5062
08 8372 0999
e-mail: info@hkaustralia.com

New Zealand: Human Kinetics
P.O. Box 80
Mitcham Shopping Centre, South Australia 5062
0800 222 062
e-mail: info@hknewzealand.com

E6718

Contents

Preface

The recent surge in the desire to reconnect to the natural world can almost be considered a social movement. Many after-school and community-based programs have been created to respond to this emerging interest, and there is no shortage in the number of quality reference books available to outdoor program leaders. However, one area lacking in quality support, and general participant involvement, is winter pursuits.

To children, winter means snow forts, sledding, and snowball fights. To many adults, on the other hand, winter is the reason to retreat to the great indoors. In fact, it's uncommon to see adults outside in winter unless they are dashing from cars to buildings, collars up, heads down. Why are so few people out and about on that perfect winter's day? Many of us seem to have forgotten how to be a part of winter life, thus restricting our activity to the gym or pursuits conducive to the other three seasons.

This guide is intended to revive the forgotten season of winter. As outdoor leaders, we are concerned that many people miss the beauty and opportunities of winter—not to mention the physical, mental, and spiritual gains realized by simply getting outside during the cold months. To lure people out into the winter landscape, we have one framing question: How can we have fun, be safe, and stay active leading others during the winter?

The winter landscape invites exploration and adventure.
© Andrew Foran

The Get-Outside Guide to Winter Activities explores a range of outdoor winter activities for people with varying interests and abilities, from walking outside in the winter to snowshoeing and skiing to extended camping expeditions. Our framework is applicable to multiage groups, settings, environments, and programs. All you need is snow!

We will show you how to help others embrace the cold, have fun, and experience the wonder of snow. Success for us will be seeing more families, schoolchildren, and adults of all ages enjoying the benefits of winter activity; freely playing in the snow; and realizing, through direct experience, the magic, adventure, and fun of winter. In this book we share ideas of how to engage with your local snowy environments and how to create programs for schoolyards, back fields, urban parks, community trails, parklands, remote trails, and wilderness areas. Every area offers numerous possibilities for exploring and playing, as long as we Get Outside (GO)!

In our work with other outdoor leaders, teachers, and camp counselors, we are often asked, "How can I lead others *out here* so they can be comfortable and safe and gain from the winter experience?" Some feel overwhelmed by the amount of planning and preparation involved in simply going for a winter jaunt—the environment dictates all! Over the years, fewer and fewer leaders have drawn on winter pursuits in their programming; as a result, fewer and fewer people have been exposed to winter activities. Winter skills, and winter memories, have been on the decline, and winter activity has been relegated to watching winter sports on TV.

Following are a few compounding reasons for this instructional gap:

- An overly technical emphasis on the skills thought to be required to participate in outdoor winter activities
- The belief that the outdoors is something to be feared rather than embraced, which is magnified during the winter
- A lack of ideas to keep groups and individuals engaged and having fun outdoors

The Get-Outside Guide to Winter Activities addresses how to teach skills and techniques as well as how to communicate to participants the benefits of the outdoors in winter. The approach is practical and user friendly, suitable for people of a variety of fitness and skill levels. You can use tried-and-tested ideas and activities in your program or for yourself, as long as you have snow. Both leaders and participants gain from being active, learning skills, having fun, engaging in activities, playing games, and connecting to the natural world during a season that defines northern living.

Winter is a part of seasonal life in many parts of the world. The ancient Greeks believed that the god Boreas ushered in the winter with cold northern winds that were a harbinger of snow; storms; sleet; and the long, dark, bleak days that last until spring. In modern times, we have resorted to hunkering down and waiting for the spring equinox to gift us with longer, brighter, warmer days. We have learned to hibernate despite all that can be experienced in snow. At no other time in history have people had access to so many places and forms of equipment to get the most out of winter. Yet we limit our time outdoors from November to April, removing ourselves from engagement with the natural world until the melt. This book can show you the way back outdoors during the winter months, and help you and those you lead stay active and create happy memories of having fun with snow.

The Get-Outside Guide to Winter Activities offers ideas, skill progressions, and games so that you and your participants can enjoy the snow once again, or for the first time. The intermediates in your group can extend their boundaries to explore more of the natural wintry world, and seasoned winter trekkers can plan and undertake snowy backcountry expeditions.

This book presents a collection of activities, from simple things to do on a hike to tactical snow games, for all participants—in urban locations, remote parks, or wilderness settings. We share planning and skill progressions, activities that require no props (or very few), age-appropriate and adaptive snow games, wintry tips based on our own winter excursions, gear requirements, and leadership suggestions. To make the material accessible to everyone, we provide conversions from metric to imperial (and vice versa); in the case of meters, if you use the imperial system, you can replace the number of meters with yards.

The contributors to this book are doers in the outdoors, winter trek leaders, and people who have embraced opportunities to get outside in winter. Our hope is that the book will inspire you to be active and connected to the natural world 12 months of the year. By following the planning and skill progressions, you can find enjoyment living in a snowbound environment; everyone can be a winter trekker. The phrase *Winter is coming* should conjure memories of sharing stories of snowy wonder around the warmth of a fire and excitement about the possibilities of winter adventures waiting to happen. Winter is here!

Rather than focus too much on the skills needed for participating in outdoor winter activities, we help you create age-appropriate activities that bring skills into action naturally and progressively, and within participants' ability ranges. The approaches, activities, and ideas can be modified to ensure that you maintain an inclusive model: Winter is for people of all abilities! We balance fun with skills and safety. Activities and suggestions for solo winter trekking are also provided for those interested in using the skills and lessons as a launching point to planning extended winter outings. A sequence of activities is presented to help you prepare participants for snowshoeing, Nordic skiing (classic cross-country, skate skiing, and backcountry), and exploratory outings such as winter day trips (from a base camp), overnight excursions (to an established camp or lodge), and winter expedition camping (establishing your own camps). Most important are the tried-and-tested activities that you can use with various age groups to keep people engaged in the snow.

Acknowledgments

There are many whom we would like to thank for their guidance, sharing, and encouragement in writing this book. To avoid leaving someone out, we felt we would say it like this: For those who have made a snowball, dug out a fort in the side of a snowbank, placed a scarf around the neighborhood snowwoman (or snowman), or stuck out their tongue to catch a floating snowflake, and those who see diamonds when walking on the crunchy fresh fallen snow under a moonlit sky, thanks for keeping the magic of winter alive!

We would also like to thank all those "kids" (young and old) who would follow us outdoors during the winter. Thank you for keeping us young at heart!

A special thanks to Mervin Parsons for sharing his collection of Inuit activities that are included within chapter 5 of this book.

The authors would also like to acknowledge the exceptional work of the Human Kinetics staff—Diana Vincer, Jacqueline Eaton Blakley, Anne E. Mrozek, Karla Walsh, Dalene Reeder, Whitney Milburn, Keith Blomberg, Laura Fitch, Jason Allen, and Kelly Hendren—for your contributions that made this book an enticing, accessible, and professional product. Thank you for your honesty, insight, and input throughout this process. We know it's not always easy working with individuals who spend little time indoors.

Preparing for Winter Fun and Adventure

Part I

Chapter 1
Getting Ready to GO

It is not easy to lead groups, let alone lead them outside. Compound this with environmental challenges such as winter weather, and the expectation on the leader is magnified. But outdoor winter fun is there to be had; you just need to know the group, know the terrain, and respect the winter weather.

Being cold outside in the winter is inevitable, but frozen and miserable—that's a leadership issue. There is being cold and then there is being chilled to the bone. A person who reaches that point will not have fun, and neither will you or the group. Your first task, then, is to build a foundation by taking steps to ensure a fun, comfortable, challenging experience for everyone.

Setting

A winter outing might be an exploration just outside a school or community center or a field trip to a local park. It might be a half-day trip, an overnight campout, or an extended expedition to a remote location. Regardless of the setting, certain considerations are important to keep in mind during the planning stage: making sure your activity matches the location, assessing risks, creating a base camp, establishing warming huts, and getting permission to use the land.

Ensuring an Activity–Location Match

It is essential to evaluate how your location will work with your activity. For example, if participants have never cross-country skied and the terrain by the school is all hills, this would not be an ideal location in which to introduce them to the sport. When planning the activity, you need to think about the necessary equipment (more about this in chapter 3), but also about the fitness level of your group. Consider these guiding questions:

- What does the group want to try first (assuming you will be together for a full winter program)?
- How much time do you have with them: one hour, one day, one week, the entire winter season?
- What type of gear can you access for each participant?
- Does anyone in the group need special consideration to maintain an inclusive learning environment?

A Snow by Any Other Name

The Inuit have many phrases for snow, including the following:

- *quanik*: falling snow
- *aputi*: snow on the ground
- *pukak*: crystalline snow on the ground
- *aniu*: snow used to make water
- *siku*: ice
- *nilak*: freshwater ice (for drinking)
- *qinu*: slushy ice by the sea

When considering location, consider both the natural features and the infrastructure of the teaching area (e.g., school or community center grounds, local park, lodge at an established base camp, wilderness area). For most group activities, the ideal setting is flat terrain with an accessible moderate slope that has no or limited obstacles. In park or wilderness areas, look for hills with varying degrees of slope (avoid extreme slopes), wooded areas, open spaces, easily accessed parkland, marked trails, a warming shelter, restrooms or pit toilets (this is huge anytime of the year), cell phone coverage, advanced support in the event of an emergency, water (yes, it might be frozen—more on this later), and snow. Finding out whether the area has adequate snow is critical for many activities. Plans laid out in November for a January excursion may be useless if winter arrives late in your area and there is no snow to speak of. Winter weather is unpredictable. In some cases, no snow = no GO. In other cases, although you can still get outside, snow activities will be limited. Regardless, even if there is some snow, is this the right type of snow for the activity? Types of snow, like snowflakes, differ markedly.

Let's consider an example of assessing activity–location match. Three of us prepared for an after-school February snowshoeing program for youth between the ages of 6 and 10 by hiking the area before winter started. These are the notes we took:

For the past two weeks, the average temperature has been –5 °C (5 °F), and the last three snowfalls have added up to 25 cm (10 in.) with drifted areas close to 35 cm (14 in.). The snow is fluffy, because there has been no rain mixing with the snowfall, and the snow packing is minimal because the cold temps have kept things dry. The municipal park managerial staff has sent us a day-use permit to snowshoe within the park boundaries (there is a private adjoining parcel of land at the far northern end), and they have agreed to open the outhouse in the center of the park, as long as we pack out any trash. The community park within a five-minute walk of our school has many looping trails that can allow for different routes for students of different ages and fitness levels, and many of the loops take us to the outbuilding that is a four-walled enclosure (open walled in summer), which is next to the outhouse. Off many of the trails is varying hilly terrain with mature hardwood and softwood trees. Three weeks ago we walked the trails and noted a huge pond past the shelter. A sizable brook on the east end runs into the pond, with several streams fanning out at the west end. The trails are all widely bridged, spanning the watercourses. We also noted that at 1.2 km (3/4 mile) from the gate on the direct trail, our cell phones were not operational. Nowhere in the park was there an open field or space for large group activities.

After surveying the location for our after-school program, we had to weigh the factors to assess its appropriateness for a snowshoeing event. Table 1.1 shows a planning guide that summarizes factors we considered in leading the group there.

TABLE 1.1 Activity–Location Match Planning Guide

Checked	Category	Rationale	Thoughts
	Warm area to start	Dry and warm place to do snowshoes and day pack checks	Open classroom connected to the gym with a mudroom leading to the back field
	Access to open spaces	Two large open spaces with adequate snow coverage at the school	For snowshoe games before our trip to the park
	Adequate snow	At least 15 cm (6 in.) for open areas; more for wooded areas	More than enough snow to cover the trails at the park and includes under-tree cover
	Access to park	Trails and access to wooded areas, varied terrain	Local park within walking distance with varied terrain (hills—gradual, moderate, and steep) and tree variety to allow us to do other activities on snowshoes
	Warming shelter	For warming breaks if needed	To store additional supplies on site: activity resources, food and drinks, backup gear
	Pit toilets	Do not have to return to school	Teach kids how to use an outhouse, bring a shovel to dig out the doorway from snow buildup, and bring extra toilet paper.
	Looping trail system that comes back to the shelter area	For snowshoeing adventures	Provide multiple activities so participants can choose their adventures.
	Access to water	Will not have to bring more water	Water will need to be purified to ensure hydration.
	Cell coverage	Spotty or poor to no coverage	Identify a spot where we can access cellular coverage.

In our preparation, we discussed each of these points as well as the age of the participants, what we knew about them, what we still needed to know about them, the games we wanted to present, the seasonal factors, and the lay of the land. Leading activities outdoors requires flexibility, creativity, innovation, and the able to work with what you have. Rather than try to force a program, you can often reach your goals by modifying and adapting to your situation.

Assessing Risk Factors

Assessing the location also involves identifying risks and what-ifs. This allows you to choose activities that are possible—and more is often possible in your own backyard than you may think! One important way to ensure the safety of your group is to make each activity age and developmentally appropriate.

The following list addresses several items in table 1.1 that are worth noting in terms of risk assessment. Two particularly important issues are water in winter and knowing an area before leading a group there.

- Water in the park presented a risk. Because this was early in the season, safe ice may have been spotty for an individual, let alone a group. Ice thickness is critical; it takes only a second for someone to wander out onto inferior ice (especially when everything is covered in snow). The outing can change to a disaster in a heartbeat if the ice gives way. Avoid activities on or near water if you have any doubt about its thickness. Knowing where water is in the park allowed us to plan activities away from the risky areas.

- The bridges spanning the stream and brook were wide enough for easy snowshoeing, and generous enough in span to prevent participants from sliding into the stream if they toe-tripped and fell. The bridge crossing the brook on the east side of the pond was railed.

- The poor cell phone coverage would affect us only during a portion of the loop trail, which was marked to allow for a simple return to the shelter.

- The warming shelter allowed for an easy retreat to a secure environment for a quick break and change of mittens or hats.

- The varied terrain allowed for activities to stay within the skill level of the group.

We discuss emergency planning in more depth in chapter 2. This general discussion helps frame risk assessment in the context of choosing a location. You cannot make a location match your program; you can only work with what is there. Planning is about knowing your group as much as it is about knowing the activity and how it will work in a particular location. You may also need to modify an activity to meet the unique needs of a group. Proper planning goes a long way in reducing the risks of a program.

Establishing a Base Camp

When it comes to setting, working out of a school or community center has a range of advantages and disadvantages. Exploring a park or a wilderness area can really accent the adventure. No matter where your activities take place, however, you need to have a base camp to retreat to. A base camp is a place to take a break from the cold and swap wet gear for dry—a place to sit and have a hot chocolate. In the preceding example, we were fortunate that an outbuilding in the center of the park was available for our group. When we do not have that possibility, we set up a portable shelter. In remote areas or wilderness reserves, groups may be able to access lodges, camps, or cottages maintained for these purposes. You may be able to book a shelter for your program, creating a bit of ease. When working in an urban area, a school site is a good base camp.

If the remote or wilderness setting does not have a shelter for a base camp, you can bring a temporary one. In chapter 9, we describe how to set up a base camp, including a heated one to use for warming and drying gear. In remote settings, accessing outside support may be challenging as a result of snowy terrain and poor or nonexistent cell phone coverage. With these types of locations, you will need to take extra care developing sound emergency plans to contact the outside world for help and to evacuate a person or the group, as well as to deal with the simple logistics of moving the group in and out. The more remote the location is, the more challenging these issues are. Remote locations up the ante for pretrip planning and, of course, required winter living and winter trekking skills.

Often, your location affords more possibilities than you might think. Activities can be adapted to target certain goals. With careful modifications, positive, fun group experiences are possible, even if the location is somewhat lacking. For example, if your wooded area does not boast sugar maple trees and you were hoping to tap trees for maple syrup, you may be able to tap birch trees, which are found in many locations. Birch syrup has a unique and interesting flavor.

Working together setting up the base camp.
© Andrew Foran

The greatest advantage to basing your program out of a school or community center is accessibility. When introducing winter pursuits to a group, having a structured base to return to is very helpful. If someone gets cold, needs a restroom break, or forgets an item, returning to the building is not onerous. Another advantage is the accessibility of stored props or materials for games and activities—you do not have to haul it all with you (more on this later—we do have solutions). Furthermore, you have a controlled environment in which to set up before venturing outside.

Bringing a group to a natural location with minimal effort creates the magic. With careful planning, you can focus on the group, not on logistics. Being immersed in nature often creates powerful experiences, even in municipal parks. Being among the trees can provide opportunities for tracking wildlife or identifying trees, and a blanket of snow provides a sense of solitude that is hard to find elsewhere.

A shelter in a natural area such as a park or reserve is ideal for a base camp. It can provide supply storage, a place to retreat to for a break from the cold, and a space to change socks and wet gear. If you are really fortunate, it may have a little woodstove to help dry and warm the group before the next mini adventure. More often than not, parks and reserves do not have many open spaces for games and activities, as would be found in a school setting. Therefore, you will need to select activities that work with the wooded terrain.

Setting Up Portable Warming Huts

As stated earlier, one of the factors in determining a location is shelter. Does the area have a warming hut or shelter? When staying on-site, this is not a concern—you can easily move a group back to base camp for a quick restroom break or snack, or to get warm. However, when expanding the program into parklands and more remote locations, you will find that some parks have permanent shelters, which are a bonus!

In some remote locations, we like to set up portable lightweight tents modeled after the classic prospector or fur trader tents. Made of lightweight duck canvas, they are easy to set up and durable for reasonable periods of time. For some programs, we leave them set up for a number of groups over the course of a couple of weeks. For extended day programs, we bring along a tent and a little woodstove—that's right, a little woodstove—to warm the tent. Once the stove is lit, the tent can get quite warm, creating the option of drying gear. These tents make great lunch spots and warming huts on an extended basis. We go into more detail about shelters in chapters 8 and 9, which address alternate shelters for day and extended winter trips.

Requesting Permission for Land Use

Accessing land to use for recreation and education is not as difficult as it might seem. If you explain clearly the purpose of the program, your use is likely to be approved. Reasons for denial include park maintenance, seasonal shutdown, and an inability to reach the private landowner. Requesting permission is about building community partnerships and establishing credibility for your program. Even though many of the residents of my community use the local golf club for snow-

FIGURE 1.1   Land use permission request letter.

[Date]

To: Mr. G. Murphy, DNR Regional Land Manager

Re: Follow-up to the phone conversation seeking permission from Department of Natural Resources, Antigonish, Nova Scotia

On behalf of the GO Winter after-school group based out of the St. Andrew's Junior School, I am formally seeking permission to access the lands by the Upper Pond of Monk's Head for our snowshoeing experience February 9 and 10, 2016. Two coleaders and I will lead 20 students on the trek. Because of the proximity to the school, we will be accessing the main trail, and there will be only one vehicle at the trailhead. We will also post the sign informing other community members that a group will be using the trails from 2:30 to 4:00 p.m. on those two days.

Permission to use these lands will allow us to fulfill our goal of exploring a natural landscape on snowshoes. We will be leading a series of activities (tree identification, animal tracking), and we will be hiding a few geocaches in advance. At the end of the program, we will remove all materials from the site as well as our own trash and any other trash we find.

We on the leadership team have spent time in the park assessing teaching locations and are aware of potential hazards and the private land that borders the north end of the park. We will not bring participants into those areas. We would like to express our gratitude to your office for opening the pit toilets for our group. Please be assured that all activities will be conducted with respect for participant safety and for the land we will be exploring. A day before the program starts, I will drop off a route card and our at-a-glance program form for your records.

Again, thank you.
Andrew Foran, TA Loeffler, and Kevin Redmond
GO Winter leaders

shoeing and skiing, I still reach out to the course manager to seek permission. This simple courtesy goes a long way in ensuring access to winter landscapes in the future. Even if the land is privately owned or under government management at the municipal, provincial or state, or federal level, people have a right to know how the land is being used and why. Figure 1.1 is a letter requesting permission to access private land; feel free to adapt it to your own purposes.

Five Gs

When planning an outdoor winter excursion of any length, we consider the five Gs—goal, group, gear, guidelines, and gain—to ensure the best experience for everyone. Are we in the right place, at the right time, with the right group, doing the right activity, with the right equipment? These questions can help keep you honest and prevent you from pushing forward with a program you are not prepared for. In the end, you want your participants to have had a positive winter experience. Following is a breakdown of the five Gs:

• **Goal.** What is the session goal? What do you want to achieve as a group? The answers help you design experiences focused on the needs of the group. Sharing your goal with the group, or even developing it together, often clarifies the purpose and boundaries of the activity and can ensure buy-in from everyone.

• **Group.** Who are your participants? What does each person bring to the group—what is each person's strength? Are there limitations that require modifications or adaptations to ensure an inclusive environment? Careful consideration in the planning stage results in selecting activities that best challenge participants and meet their developmental stage. You may want to consult with an individual, his or her parents or caregivers, or a teaching assistant to learn what you can do to best support the person's involvement in the program. Most people know what they want or need; they just need to be asked.

• **Gear.** What equipment is available for the group? What resources can you draw on to meet your goal? When selecting equipment, inspect for wear tear and provide needed tune-ups. The last thing you need is a gear failure that prevents full participation or leads to an injury. That being said, even gear in good condition can break. Be sure to carry the required tools and parts for quick fixes in the field. Most often, a good maintenance program prevents mishaps—but not always.

• **Guidelines.** What are your guidelines for safe participation in your activity? What expectations and standards do you have for participants? Be sure to take the time to inform and explain your guidelines to the group, as well as to the entire leadership team and all chaperones. A positive experience begins with making sure everyone knows what to do to keep the activity safe.

• **Gain.** What growth do you hope to see in your participants as a result of your program? Will your plan help move them in that direction? The gains we have articulated for our programs include increased activity time, positive social engagement, individual growth, group bonding, and connections to the natural winter world. In short, we hope our participants grow and come to appreciate the forgotten season of winter and want to continue their snowy adventures with friends and family.

At this stage, we have considered the location, the program activities, and the people in the group. Being knowledgeable in these three areas will aid in program development. The less you know about the participants at this point, the more conservative your program plan needs to be. The more you know, the freer you are to expand your offering. By the conclusion of the session, you want people to have had fun, been challenged, and grown personally—you want them to be glad they came and want to return. If you have not had a chance to get to know your participants before the start of the program, you can begin with icebreakers, get-to-know-you activities, and snow games (described in part II), or speak with the organizers (parents, teachers) as much as possible.

Planning and Preparation

Planning and preparation (P&P) creates an outdoor foundation in the schoolyard, at the local park, or as part of a camp experience. The bottom line is that you must maintain a consistent, solid P&P practice: A poorly planned winter excursion is a reflection of its leaders. There is very little room for half measures when leading people outdoors during the winter. The good news is that when the little things are in place, you can focus on delivering quality experiences.

Winter by nature presents environmental challenges: cold, wet snow, rain, freezing rain, and wind chill. The seasonal impact is magnified by the possibility of cold-related injuries when leaders and participants are not prepared. Being outdoors in winter is fun; you just need to be a bit more on your game. Know your group, know the terrain, and respect the weather.

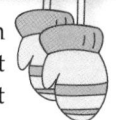

> ### The Color of Snow
>
> Snow is made up of ice particles, which are of course colorless. Snow usually has a white appearance because light does not pass through it easily and is reflected. Sometimes deep snow can appear to be blue because the layers of snow create a filter for the light, causing more red light to be absorbed than blue light.

At this stage of program planning, you want to know the following:

- What is the purpose of the lesson?
- Who are the participants?
- What activity (or activities) do participants want to do?
- Do participants have any special interests based on the terrain or prior knowledge and experiences?
- Will we be on the school or community center site or off-site?
- Will transportation be arranged?
- Will we need park permits and permission to use an existing shelter?
- Are we responsible for food and drinks?
- Who is taking care of what?

In addition to these questions, you will also need to consider the following issues in your planning:

- **Risks.** Do you have first aid training (emergency, standard, or wilderness and remote first aid) to support the health of your participants? Do you know the medical conditions of your participants and, if required, adult chaperones? What risks are present in the area? School sites—which offer an existing shelter base and easier access for 911 response—require a different kind of risk assessment than parks or camps do.

- **Equipment.** Do you have the equipment needed for ensuring a positive and comfortable learning experience? To make sure participants are prepared, send home a preparation list that includes the appropriate clothing and footwear (including a change of clothes), drinks, snacks, lunch, and any special considerations.

- **Weather.** We know you cannot control the weather, but you should have a good idea of what to expect in terms of rain, snow, sun, and so forth.
- **Terrain.** It's always a good idea to do a site examination of the terrain before the program. Clear away obstructions, and note areas that could lead to injuries (e.g., hollows, stumps, or obstructions that may be covered in snow if you are leading a running game, and even dog waste).
- **Behavior and group dynamics.** Before the program begins, communicate to the group your expectations for their behavior, and note group dynamics in advance if possible. Note who may need additional support outdoors (from you, your teaching assistants, or chaperones). Also review a few key etiquette practices regarding respect for the environment (e.g., Leave No Trace).
- **Shelter.** Do you need to bring a shelter to support the lesson (e.g., a portable base camp, a tarp for rain or snowfall), or does the site have an outbuilding?
- **Maps and routes.** If your program is taking place off-site, do you have maps? Be sure to identify walking routes, and determine an evacuation route in case of emergencies.
- **Plan B.** Having a backup plan is a must outdoors.
- **Itinerary.** Leave a trip itinerary with the program administration team, along with your outdoor instructional plans.
- **Roles and responsibilities.** If your program requires additional adult supervision (e.g., parent helpers), conduct a preprogram meeting to define roles and responsibilities. This puts everyone on the same page and avoids communication issues later on.

Duty Roster

For off-site, complex outings, a duty roster—a list of tasks with people assigned to each one—is a must. In our groups, we choose one person to make sure all tasks are completed. Table 1.2 shows an example of a duty roster.

TABLE 1.2   Duty Roster

Name	Task	Deadline	Comments	Completed
Andrew	Collect permission forms	January 21	Forms were passed out two weeks before the trip.	
Kevin	Collect medical forms	January 18	New forms are needed to keep current. Last trip was over three months ago.	
TA	Menu checks	January 23	Establish snack groups and ensure balanced meals.	
Andrew	Group gear check	January 11	Two-burner stove is not working properly. GPS batteries are low.	
Kevin	Group first aid kit check	January 20	Replace small bandages. Restock moleskin.	
TA	Participant gear check	January 24	Three participants did not have all the required gear; they are borrowing needed equipment before the next check.	

Creating and using a duty roster can help you develop consistent trip planning practices and strengthen and expand your outdoor leadership skills.

Key Forms

Some schools and organizations have their own planning procedures and forms. In addition, you should have your own forms that cover important issues. We realize that many teachers want to just get outside, but due diligence is required regardless of where the GO program takes place. Of course, the kinds of forms you use, and the number, will depend on the program you are leading. This section addresses two forms that we have found very useful: the at-a-glance form and the informed consent form.

At-a-Glance Form The at-a-glance form provides a quick overview of the event. We have found that it helps us stay organized with the paperwork (which can be overwhelming) and accountable to the P&P process—no shortcuts. Keep in mind that this form is a quick check to help you organize the key pieces; it should not be the only paperwork supporting your session. Because each program has unique features, you can adapt this form to include other information you may require. We have found it helpful to assign each group a color to facilitate quick check-ins.

Each leader and chaperone should have a copy of the at-a-glance form, in case groups are separated during some activities. A copy should also be left with an administrator or other responsible person within your program, so they know where to find you. Table 1.3 shows an at-a-glance form.

Informed Consent Form Requesting permission is about building relationships, doing things right, and establishing credibility for your program. There are two essential permissions that need to be obtained: parent or caregiver permission and land use permission, if necessary (discussed earlier). This section addresses the informed consent form, which helps develop the relationship with the adults who care for the children in your program. If your participants are adults, you should use an informed consent form to remind the leadership team of the core priorities, review the safety plan, and make sure the participants understand the program purpose—the five Gs. Figure 1.2 is a generic permission form and information letter we send home when leading youth. (See figure 2.3 for an example of the medical information form mentioned in the letter.)

Equipment

Every outdoor winter excursion, from a walk or snowshoe around school grounds to an extended camping trip, has unique equipment needs. Equipment for specific types of programs is discussed in more detail in later chapters. This section is an overview to get you thinking about the equipment you will need for your program(s).

Equipment Checks Regardless of the group, the type of trip, or the terrain, no outdoor lesson should proceed without a few equipment checks on school grounds or off-site. These include both going over lists and performing hands-on

TABLE 1.3 At-a-Glance Form

Activity	Leaders and participants	Preparation
Departure date and time: Arrival date and time:	Blue group leader: Blue group participant names and phone numbers 1. 2. 3. 4. Green group leader: Green group participant names and phone numbers 1. 2. 3. 4. Red group leader: Red group participant names and phone numbers 1. 2. 3. 4.	Duty roster complete: Pretrip meeting dates 1. 2. 3. 4. Outstanding items 1. 2. 3. 4.
Emergency procedures: Safety plan checked (date): General comments: Emergency contact and phone number: Final weather checked (date): Trip outlook Day 1: Day 2:	First-aiders: Medical forms checked: Participants and chaperones with first aid skills: First aid kit checked (date): Kit carrier:	Equipment check Group gear (date): Participant gear (date): Menu checked (date): Map numbers: Route card checked: Activity card checked:

examinations of the equipment. Following are four categories of equipment you should check:

- **First aid kit.** Contents should be checked and restocked and sealed with an electrical tie so that you know whether it has been opened (so important when sharing within a school). Make sure you have all current participant medical forms.
- **Group gear.** Group gear is equipment that the program supplies. (Pulks, for example, are not a common household item.) Group gear should be clean, of assorted sizes to fit the age group, and in good repair—field ready.
- **Leader gear.** Leader gear is what a GO leader needs to take care of their group. Leader gear can include a portable shelter, GPS unit, water purification system, extra clothes that fit the largest person in the group, resources, and supplies required for the activities.
- **Participant gear.** Participants should have all the items on the list that was sent home with the informed consent form. (See the Basic Gear section in chapter 3 for a list of needed participant equipment.)

Leader Pack One nonnegotiable leader practice is maintaining the leader pack. This pack contains essential items for leading groups in winter activities both on-site and off-site. As always, what goes into a leader pack should be adapted to seasonal realities and the type of activity you are leading. Everything in the leader pack should be checked to ensure that it is in optimal condition. Following are items to consider for your leader pack. Obviously, many will not be needed for simple on-site excursions, but they can get you thinking about what may be next!

- Day pack with a capacity between 30 and 50 liters (1,830 and 3,051 cu in.) that has a degree of water resistance. Consider investing in a pack rain cover or small tarp to wrap it in. Remember, this is not just for you. You will be carrying backup gear to take care of participants and, most likely, supplies needed for activities in the field, along with other essentials.
- First aid kit appropriate for the size of the group. If it is a basic one, you may need to add items such as extra moleskin for snowshoeing (blister prevention or care) or hot packs for cold hands while cross-country skiing.
- Map case large enough for the maps
- Compass and GPS unit
- Satellite communication system (e.g., SPOT or inReach) for areas with spotty cell service. This allows administrators and parents to follow your progress throughout the day with the tracking feature.
- Closed-cell foam pad, three-quarter or full length, for sitting on and to use if a participant needs to rest
- Tarp for making a shelter (3 by 3.5 m plastic, or a nylon guide tarp). For extended programs in the field, we use a huge nylon guide tarp (5 by 5 m). This gives participants a place to do assigned field work.
- Bothy bag: an instant shelter made of nylon

FIGURE 1.2 Informed consent form.

[Date]

Dear Parents and Caregivers,

Thank you for your interest in the GO Winter program, which educates and leads children and youth in winter pursuits to guide them in being active all season long, especially during the winter. GO is about promoting active living, having fun, and exploring the natural landscape of our community during winter. GO is also about learning certain winter skills and being safe, as we promote the importance of being physically active at [insert school or community center name].

GO Winter will take place at [location] on [dates]. Each session will be supervised by an adult leader, and for this after-school session it will be [name]. This person will oversee the entire program and may have the support of other leaders called crew leaders (CLs). For this session the CLs will be [names]. All of our youth groups are called GO crews; during the first session, your child will be assigned a crew. Leaders will be working with your child in a small-group setting.

Please provide an emergency contact name and number; have your child turn in this form and the medical information form no later than three days before the start of the program.

If there is anything that you feel is pertinent for us to know about your child, please contact us before the program starts. Also, please ensure that your child has the necessary materials and the outdoor gear listed on the equipment list you will find in this package. We want students to be comfortable and have fun, and a positive step toward reaching this goal is being dressed appropriately, having a snack [optional if this is being provided], and if needed, bringing personal medication to every session.

If you have any questions regarding the GO Winter program, please contact [name and contact information]. Please be prompt in picking up your child at the end of the session; if your child is expected to go home alone, please communicate that arrangement clearly. We thank you again for your interest in the GO Winter program and look forward to sharing in active learning sessions that will guide your child to becoming healthy and safe all year long!

Yours in active living,

_____

[school or community center name]

Permission Form

I, _____, grant permission for my child, _____, to participate in the GO Winter program described in the information letter for parents and caregivers.

Date: _____

Signature of parent or caregiver: _____

Home contact number: _____

Cell phone number: _____

Name and contact information of parent or caregiver collecting the participant:

- - - - - -CUT - - - - - - - - - CUT- - - - - - - - -CUT - - - - - - -CUT - - - - - - - -CUT - - - - - - -

The following is for your information. PLEASE SAVE.

Location: _____

Drop-off time: _____

Pickup time: _____

Special considerations: _____
_____
_____

You may contact [program coordinator name] at [phone number] if you have any questions regarding the program. The following are the coleaders for GO Winter program:

_____

_____

_____

Requirements

1. Participants must be dressed appropriately for outdoor winter activity.

2. Participants are required to bring a complete set of backup clothes and an extra hat and mittens.

3. Participants are required to bring their own water bottles and snacks.

4. Participants must adhere to the leaders' instructions regarding safety and fair play.

5. Participants must have all listed equipment in their packs. We suggest packing with them so they know what they have and where it is in their packs.

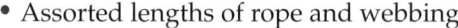

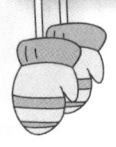

> ### Brrr . . . Be Careful Out There!
>
> In the United States, winter cold is responsible for twice as many deaths as summer heat.

- Assorted lengths of rope and webbing
- Headlamp
- Repair kit with extra batteries, tools, parts to fix gear (snowshoes, bindings, toboggans and pulks)
- Pot, stove, and fuel. Dehydrated soup makes for a hot, healthy drink in the field.
- Thermos filled with hot water (saves time if a quick warm drink is needed)
- Matches in a waterproof container, fire starters
- Water filtration system and a backup, or water purification tablets
- Change of clothes large enough to fit the largest person in the group in a waterproof sack, including extra mittens, hats, and socks
- Rain gear
- Water bottle, snacks, seasonal hat, sunscreen, lip balm
- Folding saw or hatchet. I have found a saw most useful; a hatchet has its place, but using it requires skill.
- Waterproof envelope to carry paperwork
- Resources for teaching the lesson
- Pulk (sled). I use a pulk to transport my leader pack and program resources. This is a sled with a homemade pole and harness system. I prefer poles over hauling ropes with a pulk because it allows me to move off a trail and navigate hills without the worry of the loaded sled chasing me down hills. Pulks can be purchased commercially, but I have found that a simple sled and some ingenuity does the job. The best part of making it yourself is that you will know how to fix it in the field if needed.

Transportation

If you are a teacher, you may be assuming that a school bus is the best way to transport your group. Consider, however, all the equipment you may need to bring. Imagine 60 pairs of skis and boots, along with poles and leader gear, sliding around on the bus floor. In many districts this manner of transportation is not allowed, even on a chartered bus, unless it has a designated cargo hold.

A logical solution would be to ask others (e.g., parent chaperones) to transport gear in cars, but conventional hatchbacks and trunks have limited capacity for moving mass amounts of equipment. If your program takes place on-site, your facility becomes the base camp; however, if you need to travel any distance and walking is not possible, you will need a van to move your gear. That being said, even if the location is within walking distance, carrying heavy pieces of equipment can drain the energy out of participants—but they will be warm!

Another small but important consideration is having a vehicle on-site in case a participant has to leave (this should be addressed in the emergency plan, and under general comments on the at-a-glance form). You will also have to consider how to transport a participant who must leave the program before the end. What are your program rules and procedures for this type of transport?

Nutrition

Good food is, quite simply, a morale booster. A well-timed snack can change everything: mood, energy level, and the all-important group attitude. Poor food choices, on the other hand, result in colder, less energetic, and less cooperative people.

When setting up a winter outdoor activity program, snacks are key. You will need to decide whether you will provide snacks or participants will bring their own (we always pack extras—someone always forgets). Be sure to consider food allergies, food sensitivities (celiac disease, lactose intolerance, diabetes), and Kosher or other dietary requirements, as well as the health benefit of any snacks supplied.

Gorp or trail mix is our all-time favorite snack. The mix we make includes dried fruit; nuts; coconut; and Smarties, M&Ms, or chocolate chips. Most organizations have a peanut-free policy, given the danger of peanuts to those who are allergic, and your program should be no different. When we are required to supply the snack, and gorp is appropriate, we fill 1-liter wide-mouth Nalgene bottles halfway or three-quarters of the way, rather than supply individual plastic baggies. The bottles get reused, and we avoid leaving trash behind. Each bottle has a carabiner so it can be clipped onto a participant's day pack. On extended trips this is a packable item. At snack time, participants open their bottles and shake some into their mouths—mittens stay on!

Another snack option is granola bars: purchased or homemade. There is no shortage of good granola recipes online. With care, a granola bar can be a quality food rather than just empty calories. When our groups snack on granola bars, we pass a small trash bag around. We expect all participants to take care of their own waste. Garbage left behind is a mark against the program and sign of poor leadership.

Fruit is our number one snack choice, but during the colder months, this can be challenging. Bananas do not hold up well outdoors in backpacks, let alone in the cold. Apples are hardy, but like oranges and grapes, they can freeze on an outing. And melons—really? We will leave you to experiment—let us know how the cantaloupe survived the trail at –10 °C (14 °F). However, when we have a facility or established base camp to retreat to for a snack, as in an afternoon program, fruit is on the menu! And despite raised eyebrows expressing doubt among all age groups, when the trough is open for business, there is rarely a piece of fruit left—someone is eating this stuff. If your budget allows, a little yogurt dip goes a long way. When working with a group for an extended period of time, don't be afraid to alter the menu. A veggie tray can go a long way, and carrots, celery, and broccoli survive the winter trail well.

Packing food for extended trips is addressed in later chapters. Suffice it to say, for now, that we prefer to travel with dried fruit in the winter: raisins, cranberries, banana chips, apples, dates, apricots—the list goes on. If the bulk store carries it, in the supply bag it goes.

During program breaks, we enjoy providing more than just water. Water is critical, and we deal with this next, but having a nice, warm drink can go a long way in lifting spirits. When possible, we encourage participants to bring a thermos filled with hot water or their favorite drink, and our leader pack has a thermos ready to go. However, sharing food and drink is fundamental in establishing a sense of community. To provide a warm beverage, you will need a quality stove, an ample pot, and water—and, of course, mugs. We provide mugs and carabiners for clipping them onto day packs. Some favorite warm beverage choices are hot chocolate (a favorite of youth), a mix of teas for adults (noncaffeinated—caffeine is a diuretic and contributes to heat loss, which not a good thing in winter temps; more on this later), warm cider (a favorite for most—trust us!), and, if the outing is a day trip with a lunch, a hearty soup.

Hydration

Accessing clean water is a trip priority. Although we request that all participants start out with a full water bottle from home, this can be consumed quickly when a person is active. Maintaining hydration with groups is challenging at the best of times, but winter makes more demands on the body. Therefore, a resupply is critical. What happens if a participant drops her water bottle because of slippery mittens and loses her water in the snow? Do you carry extra water in? (This is not wise, because of the sheer weight of liquids.) Perhaps you could transport water via sled or pulk. Remember, though, that water in jugs will freeze. Thus, accessing water from natural sites might be your best option.

All natural water sources must be considered suspect for contaminants; thus all water needs to be treated for health reasons. You do not want your participants ingesting microorganisms such as parasites, pathogens, and bacteria and becoming sick. Understanding the water source is essential. Does it run through farmlands where fertilizer runoff may be an issue, or through an industrial site or busy roadway, where chemical leachate may find its way into the water?

Table 1.4 compares methods of treating water in the field. Regardless of the method you select, make sure to check the instructions. As leaders, we know the importance of hydration for health and performance in the outdoors, especially during winter. We plan for having to treat water for our participants, knowing that dehydration is one of the leading causes of fatigue and accidents in outdoor pursuits.

Managing Groups Outside in Winter

Obviously, we are going to open this section with the admonition to keep your groups well hydrated and schedule water and snack breaks to keep energy levels up. This is just good practice.

You may remember from the at-a-glance form that we suggest breaking groups up into smaller, more manageable groups identified by color. This helps you do check-ins. During your time outside, you are responsible for monitoring the health and temperature of your participants—their comfort. You should teach signs and symptoms of frostbite and hypothermia before both day trips and extended trips

TABLE 1.4 Comparison of Methods for Treating Water

Treatment method	Pros	Cons	Practicality
Water filter	• Popular • Fairly reliable; most models are easy to maintain in the field. • Can treat volumes of water; check for suitability for groups vs. personal use.	• Can break in the field. • Can be expensive for consistent program use. • Can require a lot of time to pump large volumes of water.	Filters can freeze and crack in winter, rendering them ineffective or useless. The most durable models are heavy.
Chemical treatment	• Most are cost effective for programs. • Can treat large quantities. • Can treat single amounts. • Simple to use (read the instructions and do the math!) • Easy to pack and light to carry	• Most products (tablets or liquid) have an expiration date. • Some products are cold delayed (treatment time depends on temperature); read the instructions and do the math! • Some products result in water tasting bad or smelling of chemicals.	The time delay in the winter can be problematic. Not everyone will do the math, so the learning curve depends on the ability to decipher the steps. Some products may not be available where you live.
Boiling Gas stove Woodstove	Reliable if you can light the heat source. You simply bring the water to a rolling boil and maintain it for the recommended long minute. By the time the water begins to boil, microorganisms cannot survive; continuing for a minute ensures that the job is done. You can use snow, but it takes some time to melt. Snow does not require a rolling boil—just enough time to melt.	Can you get the fire going and keep it going? Do you want to be lugging in liquid fuel for the stove (liquids are heavy!). Hot water has to cool if participants are looking for a cold drink—think snow!	You will always have a supply of hot water if your heat source is effective. However, there is a time issue. If you need water now, this method is not instant; participants may not be willing to wait.

and encourage participants to be responsible for one another; but, in the end, you are responsible for your group.

A cold person will require more motivation to participate, so keep your people moving, keep them warm, and make sure they're having fun. A simple way to prevent the funk (*I'm cold . . . let me sit here . . . I'm cold . . . I want to go home . . . I'm cold . . . no, I don't want to do this now*) is to avoid downtime. If possible, do the gear explanation and fitting inside; dry fit, warm fit is good practice for any outdoor activity. Participants can practice putting on the gear, make needed adjustments, and know what needs to be done to be snow ready. You can help youth with small hands fine-tune heel straps or pole straps, or teach them how the bindings work or how to lash gear onto a sled or pulk. Remember, this is just as much about learning as it is about being active—the two support each other. We call this the *warm fit* stage. Keep in mind that you will still have a few adjustments to make outdoors. When this happens, smile, make a joke, and lend a helping hand. Two adjustments is not a big deal; 22 is downtime!

When people stand around too long outdoors, focus drops, gear-fitting issues emerge (delaying active involvement even more), and you will lose the group. Then you will have to work even harder to bring them back to the proper state of mind. Cold and downtime do not mix. When we get outdoors with our groups, we want to be moving with purpose. We recommend keeping the five Gs in mind: goal, group, gear, guidelines, and gain. To provide meaningful activities that are fun and have a purpose, make sure your people are moving, not standing.

That being said, the P&P must take transitions into account. When an instant activity (e.g., a snow tagging game) has run its course, you need to know where to go next. The next activity should be set up in advance. In our groups, I may run one activity with TA, while Kevin sets up the next. TA and Kevin then run that activity, while I set up the next. If I am on my own, I try to set these up in advance of the group's arrival. In short, I want to maximize being active on the snow, not standing on the snow.

This P&P consideration also applies to setting up activity stations at the facility or along the trail. When assessing an area, consider what you can do to ensure that it is safe and that you use the landscape to best advantage. Do not leave this to chance—make a plan and work the plan, because the outdoors has its own agenda. From activity to activity, know the flow, adjust if needed, modify if required, and consider transitions from station to station to prevent the dreaded downtime. This is about GO, not wait!

Summary

A winter trip can offer adventure and provide youth an opportunity to explore nature in a season when most people have cut themselves off from nature. To ensure a winter outing is optimized, the leader needs to plan with the following mantra in mind: Take care of the little things before they become a big problem later on! For a leader to keep the details in check, the duty roster and at-a-glance form become an excellent starting point. However, solid home communication is essential in ensuring participants arrive prepared. If unprepared, they will be cold, and it's hard to motivate an ice-cold group. The leaders need to do their part, with a bombproof leader pack and a solid plan; knowing the plan well allows the leaders to turn their attention to the participants and the next activity. A well-planned outing takes effort, and the details should not be left to chance; we want people enjoying the snow!

Chapter 2
Safety and Risk Management

One thread throughout this book is embracing winter. Snow, ice, cold, blizzards, and the environment associated with these features offer a different experience from temperate conditions. At times the experience can be intense, but soon participants realize that they can be comfortable and enjoy activities in adverse conditions. In most cases this realization will not occur without active preparation by the leader and participants and effective communication.

Embracing winter involves expecting and even hoping for winter conditions. To ensure a safe and enjoyable experience, you need to know what to expect in winter environments and match this knowledge with your participants' abilities, knowledge, expectations, preparedness, and sense of personal and group responsibility. You are responsible for gearing up participants; completing the activity plan; doing the weather check and predicting weather in the field; anticipating and knowing what to do in adverse conditions; understanding wind chill, hypothermia, and the treatment for hypothermia; ensuring cold weather safety; managing risk, and developing and using emergency plans. All of these things are addressed in this chapter.

Winter conditions are the attraction, reward, and risk inherent in getting outside in winter. Your personal preparations in conjunction with knowing and preparing your participants, and your ability to balance the risks and rewards of going outside for winter play, all contribute to a safe and rewarding experience for you and your participants alike.

Assessing Environmental Conditions

Although weather forecasting has improved significantly in recent years, local conditions and the forecast can change. Before heading out, check the local weather and get a prediction for the duration of your trip. Educate yourself about the types of weather common in the area at the time you will be out there.

> ### *Snow Bloomers*
>
> You can't expect to see many plants blooming while you're out in the snow . . . but if you happen to be trekking in East Asia, you might come across a beautiful Chinese plum flowering in the winter!

Always prepare a plan B in case of changing weather conditions, keeping in mind the group's abilities, the location, snow, and other related factors. When out on an adventure, do not ignore nature's signs of oncoming weather, and plan to take appropriate precautions should the weather turn bad. Make sure you and your charges are dressed and packed for the unexpected.

Although technology is a great aid to weather prediction, local microclimates and conditions can vary significantly from the available general weather forecast. With this in mind, a variety of strategies for weather forecasting (e.g., weather lore, atmospheric pressure) can help you in the field. Making weather forecasting part of the group's responsibility can also add to the outdoor experience. A basic knowledge of weather forecasting also contributes to informed decision making.

Weather Lore

Throughout history, farmers, sailors, and shepherds have relied on weather lore. There are many examples of lore, but not all are reliable. Following are some of the most trusted, which can easily be used during outdoor adventures:

- Red sky at night, sailors delight; red sky at morning, sailors take warning.
- When the wind is in the east, 'tis neither good for man nor beast.
- The more cloud types present, the greater the chance of rain or snow.
- No weather's ill if the wind be still.
- A halo around the sun, expect precipitation soon.
- The sharper the blast, the sooner 'tis past.
- The higher the clouds, the better the weather.
- When seagulls fly to land, a storm is at hand.

Clouds

There are many kinds of clouds—high, medium, and low clouds, and clouds that grow vertically. All clouds have possible weather implications; table 2.1 is a guide to cloud types and their weather indicators, and figure 2.1 illustrates how the different cloud types appear in the sky. You can use this information to engage participants in identifying and predicting local conditions, and also to predict the weather yourself. To add an educational component to your excursion, consider maintaining a weather observation log and asking participants questions such as the following: What is the relationship between cloud cover and temperature? What is the relationship between cloud type and atmospheric pressure? What do changes in cloud types indicate about the weather?

Atmospheric Pressure

Atmospheric pressure is the weight of the air above the point of measurement; it is measured with a barometer and sometimes referred to as barometric pressure.

TABLE 2.1   Cloud Types and Associated Weather

Cloud groups	Cloud types	Weather indicator
High clouds Above 18,000 ft (5,486 m)	Cirrus: long, thin, wispy Cirrocumulus: small, rounded puffs Cirrostratus: sheetlike and thin	Generally indicate good weather, but a possibility of a change in 12 to 24 hours.
Medium clouds 6,500 to 18,000 ft (1,981 to 5,486 m)	Altocumulus: grayish-white Altostratus: gray or blue-gray	Usually form ahead of storms that could be thunderstorms, rainstorms, or snowstorms.
Low clouds Up to 6,500 ft (1,981 m)	Stratus: uniformly gray and cover the entire sky Stratocumulus: low, puffy, and gray Nimbostratus: dark gray and ragged	Clouds can turn from fog to rain or snow.
Vertically growing clouds	Cumulonimbus: anvil-like shape	Heavy rain, snow, hail, lightning, or tornadoes

Data from BoatSafe.com, http://boatsafe.com/kids/weather1.htm.

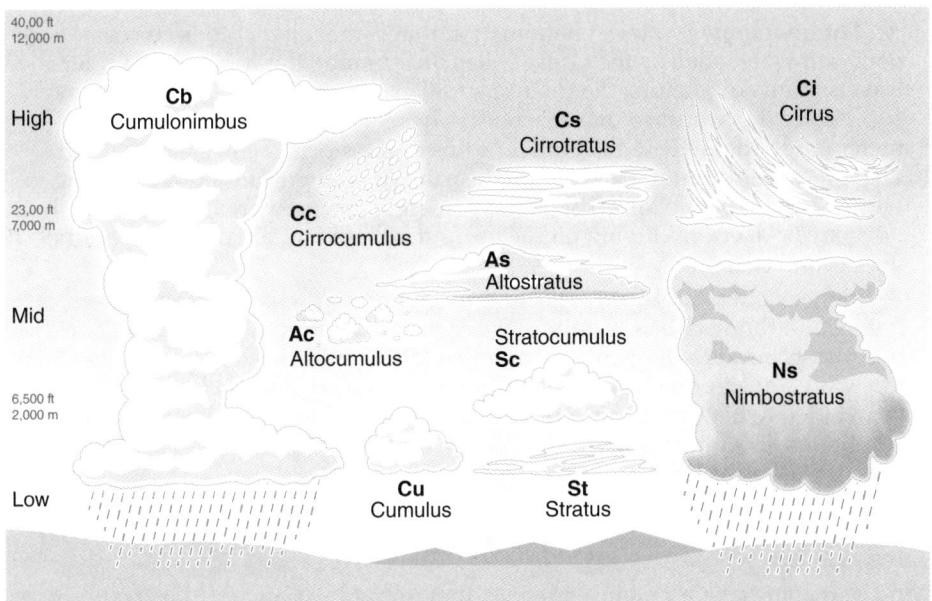

FIGURE 2.1   Types of clouds.

Illustration by Valentin de Bruyn / Coton, http://commons.wikimedia.org/wiki/File:Cloud_types_en.svg, under the terms of the Creative Commons Attribution-ShareAlike 3.0 Unported license (CC BY-SA 3.0): https://creativecommons.org/licenses/by-sa/3.0/deed.en

What If You Get Stuck in Bad Weather?

Being outdoors, as alluring as it can be, can also present unpredictable risks. As an outdoor leader, you should know what to do if your group is caught out in events such as thundersnow, blizzards, and other weather bombs.

Moisture in the air increases the weight of the air. The heavier the air is, the lower the atmospheric pressure is and the higher the probability of precipitation is. Low atmospheric pressure generally indicates that clouds and precipitation are on the way. High atmospheric pressure generally indicates that a clear day is approaching. Today, watches and small gadgets that can measure atmospheric pressure are available, but they can be expensive. For example, the Kestrel pocket weather meter ranges in price from approximately $200 to $400, depending on the model. This particular device is a recommended item for the leader pack because of the extensive variety of data available, depending on the model: temperature, wind speed, wind chill, wet bulb temperature, heat index, dew point, altitude, relative humidity, and atmospheric/barometric pressure. Regular weather monitoring improves one's ability to recognize change and trending; such information is valuable to the leader in making informed decisions.

Understanding atmospheric pressure heightens our awareness of temperature changes and potential weather systems. High atmospheric pressure with clear skies, day or night, is often associated with cooler temperatures because the earth's blanket of cloud cover is absent. Low cloud cover is usually associated with warming temperatures because a thick blanket of clouds retains the earth's heat. Low atmospheric pressure always accompanies weather systems such as heavy snowfall and blizzards.

- **Thundersnow** is a rare phenomenon that is most likely to occur near large bodies of water such as the Great Lakes. In summer, the sound of thunder travels many kilometers; the intense snow in a thundersnow event, however, suppresses the sound so that it is normally heard only within a 3- to 5-kilometer (approximately 2- or 3-mile) radius of the storm. Hence, you should take precautions immediately upon hearing or seeing thunder or lightning in winter. Do not be the tallest object; if you are in an open area, move into a less open area. Also, avoid lying on the ground, where you are prone to conducting ground currents.
- In the event of a **blizzard**, try to find shelter that will protect you from falling and flying debris. Coniferous forests are better protection than deciduous forests because they are less prone to falling branches and trees. The birch tree with a dead branch is known as a widow maker, and such hazards should be avoided. Quinzhee snow shelters also offer excellent protection in blizzard conditions. (See the quinzhee-building activity in chapter 5.)

Wind Chill

Wind and cold have a chilling effect as they draw heat away from the body, especially in areas of exposed skin. Understanding the combination of cool or cold temperature and wind is essential to your ability to plan for fun and mitigate the risks associated with winter environments. Not understanding wind chill can put all group members at risk.

The apparent temperature, or wind chill, is based on how the body's exposed skin senses cold when air temperature and wind speed are combined. In most areas of the world, wind chill is presented as a chart or table: for example, Australia uses degrees Centigrade: www.bom.gov.au/info/thermal_stress; and the United States, degrees Fahrenheit: www.nws.noaa.gov/om/winter/windchill.shtml. Other Web sources provide a calculator into which you input wind speed and temperature to determine wind chill. You can use either method (from a reputable provider such as your national weather office) to determine wind chill.

Using a chart like that shown in figure 2.2 can help you assess the danger presented by wind chill. Finding the air temperature and moving to the line corresponding with your wind speed brings you to the wind chill. For example, a temperature of 0 °C (32 °F) with a wind speed of 25 kilometers per hour (15 mph) indicates a wind chill of –6 °C (21 °F). Note that the darker the color in the chart, the higher the hazard and risk to participants.

Dangers and Variances Associated With Wind Chill

Biologically, the very young and very old have less ability to manage or tolerate the cold effect resulting from wind chill. Less body fat means less insulation and increased heat loss. Wind increases the body's loss of heat.

Loss of heat from exposed skin can result in frostnip, a superficial cooling of the skin that does not result in cellular or tissue damage, or frostbite, which does cause cellular or tissue damage. Indicators of such conditions include a white, waxy appearance on the skin surface as the skin and surrounding tissues freeze, thus preventing blood (providing heat and oxygen/gas transfer) from circulating.

A second risk associated with wind chill is hypothermia, a lowering of the core body temperature that can result in death. When the body begins to cool, it shuts down or minimizes circulation to the extremities to maintain core body temperature. If the person is sweating or wet, the heat loss from wind chill is accelerated, creating a potentially deadly circumstance.

Preparing for and Dealing With Wind Chill

As a leader planning for activity outside in winter, you need to know the safe limits for exposure to wind chill. As a general guide, a wind chill of –12 °C (10 °F) is the cutoff for younger children and youth who are not fully developed; the proposed limit for participants who are fully developed (i.e., developed adolescents and adults) is –15 °C (5 °F). In general, the developing body has less fat reserves to serve as insulation and a higher metabolism that is better suited to giving off heat than conserving heat. The fully developed body has a slower metabolism and added fat insulation and thus is more adapted to conserving heat. These thresholds should be considered when planning any outdoor excursion. Following are other considerations:

- Is the area protected from or exposed to wind? If you have the choice of an exposed meadow or a forest trail, choose the forest, which will dissipate much of the wind.
- How close are you to a warm exit? If your activity is immediately outside a school or community building that you can use for intermittent warming, this reduces but does not eliminate the risk of wind exposure.
- What is your direction of travel relative to the wind direction? In cold, windy conditions, whenever possible, plan your route to travel with the

Environment Canada Wind Chill Chart

Actual Air Temperature T_{air} (°C)

Wind Speed $V_{10\,m}$ (km/h)	5	0	−5	−10	−15	−20	−25	−30	−35	−40	−45	−50
5	4	−2	−7	−13	−19	−24	−30	−36	−41	−47	−53	−58
10	3	−3	−9	−15	−21	−27	−33	−39	−45	−51	−57	−63
15	2	−4	−11	−17	−23	−29	−35	−41	−48	−54	−60	−66
20	1	−5	−12	−18	−24	−30	−37	−43	−49	−56	−62	−68
25	1	−6	−12	−19	−25	−32	−38	−44	−51	−57	−64	−70
30	0	−6	−13	−20	−26	−33	−39	−46	−52	−59	−65	−72
35	0	−7	−14	−20	−27	−33	−40	−47	−53	−60	−66	−73
40	−1	−7	−14	−21	−27	−34	−41	−48	−54	−61	−68	−74
45	−1	−8	−15	−21	−28	−35	−42	−48	−55	−62	−69	−75
50	−1	−8	−15	−22	−29	−35	−42	−49	−56	−63	−69	−76
55	−2	−8	−15	−22	−29	−36	−43	−50	−57	−63	−70	−77
60	−2	−9	−16	−23	−30	−36	−43	−50	−57	−64	−71	−78
65	−2	−9	−16	−23	−30	−37	−44	−51	−58	−65	−72	−79
70	−2	−9	−16	−23	−30	−37	−44	−51	−58	−65	−72	−80
75	−3	−10	−17	−24	−31	−38	−45	−52	−59	−66	−73	−80
80	−3	−10	−17	−24	−31	−38	−45	−52	−60	−67	−74	−81

where

T_{air} = Actual Air Temperature in °C

$V_{10\,m}$ = Wind Speed at 10 metres in km/h (as reported in weather observations)

Notes:

1. For a given combination of temperature and wind speed, the wind chill index corresponds roughly to the temperature that one would feel in a very light wind. For example, a temperature of −25°C and a wind speed of 20 km/h give a wind chill index of −37. This means that, with a 20 km/h and a temperature of −25°C, one would feel as if it were −37°C in a very light wind.
2. Wind chill does *not* affect objects and does *not* lower the actual temperature. It only describes how a human being would feel in the wind at the ambient temperature.
3. The wind chill index does *not* take into account the effect of sunshine. Bright sunshine may reduce the effect of wind chill (make it feel warmer) by 6 to 10 units.

Frostbite Guide

Low risk of frostbite for most people
Increasing risk of frostbite for most people within 30 minutes of exposure
High risk for most people in 5 to 10 minutes of exposure
High risk for most people in 2 to 5 minutes of exposure
High risk for most people in 2 minutes of exposure or less

FIGURE 2.2 Wind chill chart.

Reprinted from Candac. Available: www.candac.ca/candac/Outreach/Teacher_Resources_Index/tri/31.pdf.

wind. Note that wind chill numbers are based on a stationary object (i.e., a person). If you are traveling into the wind, your speed adds to the impact of wind speed on exposed skin, making the apparent temperature (wind chill) colder than what appears in the wind chill table.

The best way to prepare for wind chill is to dress appropriately for the conditions, with one added caveat: cover as much exposed skin as possible. When possible, alter the body's orientation to the wind direction to avoid continuous exposure of skin to the oncoming wind. Also, maintain a pace that keeps people warm while avoiding sweating.

Warning: A calm winter day can turn into a bitterly cold day if the wind picks up. Always plan and prepare for the what-if!

Dehydration and Hypothermia

Every leader and participant should be aware of the dangers of dehydration and hypothermia and how to mitigate the risks. In most cases of hypothermia, dehydration is occurring simultaneously. Cold weather acclimatization is challenging but essential for minimizing the risk of hypothermia. Maintaining a moderate body temperature while avoiding excessive temperatures that can precipitate hypothermia requires good preparation, appropriate dress, and constant monitoring, and it is aided by experience. Remaining hydrated is equally important in reducing risk.

Dehydration

Dehydration impairs the body's ability to maintain normal functions. The general perception of dehydration is its association with warm weather; however, it is more hazardous in the cold. The reason for this, in part, is that the body does not crave fluids or sense thirst in cold weather the way it does in warm weather. Most bodily functions and processes are designed to protect the body. The body's reaction to cold is no exception. When the body senses cold, peripheral blood vessels constrict to maintain core temperature (the skin's surface becomes pale as a result of restricted blood flow). The constriction of blood vessels increases blood pressure, which in the kidneys results in increased urination and thus fluid loss. The body also loses significant amounts of fluids through respiration (consider the condensation on glass when you exhale in the cold) and through sweat. Any rise in body temperature results in sweat and fluid loss. In cold conditions, and especially with proper dress layers, sweat is wicked away from the skin; hence, the person may be less aware of fluid loss. To minimize the risk of dehydration, consider the following in your practice:

Try This

Turn on a fan and stand in front of it. You will feel colder because of the wind cooling your skin, but the temperature in the room has not changed. You cannot make the room any colder, no matter how high you turn up the fan. Similarly, no matter how strong the wind blows, the temperature of the air outside does not change. Now dab some water on your skin and stand in front of the fan again. The wet skin will feel much colder than dry skin does. This demonstrates how important it is to stay dry when outdoors in cold and windy conditions.

Reprinted, by permission, from Environment Canada and Climate Change, 2015, *Wind chill - The chilling facts.* Available: www.ec.gc.ca/meteo-weather/default.asp?lang=En&n=5FBF816A-1#table1.

- Educate all participants about the silent nature of dehydration in the cold and the importance of regular fluid intake, even when they think it is not needed

- Monitor participants' dress to prevent overdressing that may contribute to sweating and excessive fluid loss. Overdressing in moderate to hard activity can result in fluid losses ranging from 1 to 2 liters (or quarts) per hour depending on the activity level and state of overdress. Your mantra should be "Sweat is evil."

- Provide frequent short stops, not long enough that people become chilled, but long enough for "water in, water out."

- Have a hydration plan, and teach participants strategies for preventing water from freezing (insulated containers stored near the body or in the middle of the pack). Set up water partners, who retrieve and return each other's water bottles from their packs. Partners should monitor each other's fluid intake and, depending on the age and experience of the participants, take responsibility for the availability of good water.

Hypothermia

Being exposed to cold with proper preparation, dress, monitoring, and maintenance can be a comfortable, enjoyable, and rewarding experience. Failure to monitor and address the hazards of exposure to cold can kill. Conditions that contribute to and often accompany hypothermia are low temperatures, dehydration, improper clothing or equipment, poor food intake, wet or damp clothes or skin, alcohol intake, fatigue, and exhaustion.

Hypothermia is a decrease in the core body temperature to a level at which normal muscle and brain functions are impaired. Hypothermia is a leading cause of death related to outdoor activities. Exposure to cold, wind, and snow without adequate clothing can lead to hypothermia. Extreme cold is not a prerequisite to hypothermia; in fact, most hypothermia occurs in cool weather. There is a real risk of hypothermia anytime you spend time outdoors in cool or cold weather. Of note is that hypothermia can occur at any temperature below body temperature—37 °C (98.6 °F). Never let yourself or a member of your group reach even the early stages of hypothermia. Always monitor each other.

To minimize the risk of hypothermia and prevent or reduce heat loss, wear warm, dry clothing and wear warm-when-wet clothing such as pile or wool and dress in layers with a wicking layer adjacent to the skin, followed by insulation layers and an outer shell to minimize the effect of wind and keep heat inside. To increase heat production, increase activity or eat sufficient amounts of carbohydrate before and during activity.

You and your participants have an equal role in reducing the risk of hypothermia. Your job is to ensure that participants are aware of cold weather activity protocols that mitigate risk, as well as to create a mood and social culture in which participants feel empowered to address cold-related concerns. Once participants are aware of hazards and how to avoid or minimize risks, they should be person-

---

The section on hypothermia is adapted, by permission, from K. Redmond, 2003, *A guide to sea kayaking Newfoundland & Labrador*. By permission of Kevin Redmond.

ally responsible for themselves and communicate with their peers and leaders when there is a concern beyond their ability or control. You must encourage open communication in addition to constantly monitoring participants' conditions, especially temperature, hydration, energy level, and mood or demeanor. Everyone should also understand the ways we lose heat so you can all take steps to reduce the effect of cold when engaged in outdoor activity.

> ## How Cold Can Cold Get?
>
> The lowest temperature ever recorded was –89.2 degrees Celsius in 1983 in Soviet Vostok Station, Antarctica.

Prevention   Understanding how a person loses heat to the environment is the first step in the prevention of hypothermia. The four ways our bodies lose heat are radiation, conduction, convection, and evaporation.

- **Radiation.** Radiant heat loss occurs only when the surrounding temperature is below 37 °C (98.6 °F). Factors important in radiant heat loss are the surface area and the temperature difference between you and your environment. Dressing appropriately reduces heat loss through radiation.

- **Conduction.** Conduction is heat loss through direct contact between objects. Heat travels from a warmer object to a colder one. Water conducts heat away from the body 25 times faster than air. Generally, conductive heat loss accounts for only about 2 percent of overall loss. However, with wet clothes, the loss is increased five times. Conductive heat loss may be minimized by using a barrier between warm body parts (e.g., insulated boots) and snow or ice.

- **Convection.** Heat is lost when air or water molecules against the surface are heated, moved away, and replaced by new molecules that are also heated. The rate of convective heat loss depends on the substance (water convection occurs more quickly than air convection) and the speed of the moving substance. Wind chill is an example of the effects of air convection. In modern clothing systems, convection occurs when warm air escapes from the layers (e.g., through vents, cuffs, or collars) and is replaced by cooler air.

- **Evaporation.** Evaporation results from the conversion of water from a liquid to a gas. Heat loss through evaporation occurs through sweating, which is the body's response to excess heat. The body sweats to maintain a humidity level of 70 percent next to the skin; in a cold, dry environment, you can lose a great deal of moisture this way. During respiration, air is heated as it enters the lungs and is exhaled with an extremely high moisture content. Recognizing the strong connections between fluid levels, fluid loss, and heat loss is important. As body moisture is lost through evaporative processes, the overall circulating volume is reduced, which can lead to dehydration. This decrease in fluid level makes the body more susceptible to hypothermia.

Signs and Symptoms   When monitoring someone (or yourself) for signs and symptoms of hypothermia, watch for the *umbles* (stumbles, mumbles, fumbles, and grumbles) that show changes in motor coordination and levels of consciousness. Following are signs and symptoms of various stages of hypothermia:

Mild: Core temperature of 37-35 °C (98-95 °F)

- Shivering
- Inability to do complex functions but can still walk and talk

Moderate: Core temperature 35-33 °C (95-92 °F)

- Dazed consciousness
- Loss of fine motor coordination, particularly in hands (e.g., cannot zip up a jacket)
- Slurred speech
- Violent shivering
- Irrational behavior
- "I don't care" attitude

Severe: Core temperature 33-30 °C (92-86 °F) and below (immediately life threatening)

- Shivering in violent waves followed by pauses
- Pauses get longer until shivering finally ceases

Treatment   The basic principle behind treating someone with hypothermia is to rewarm the person to conserve the heat he has and replace the body fuel he is burning up to generate heat. Reduce heat loss by replacing wet clothing with dry, adding additional layers of clothing, providing shelter, and adding fuel and fluids to help the body generate heat from within. Increased physical activity can help in mild stages. External heat can be from fire or another heat source such as another body.

Foods high in carbohydrate are best for quick energy intake, especially for those with mild cases of hypothermia. Carbohydrate is quickly released into the bloodstream for a sudden, brief heat surge. On the other hand, protein and fat are released slowly and give off heat over a longer period. Hot liquids provide calories plus a heat source, sugars are a source of carbohydrate, and gorp (good ol' raisins and peanuts) contains carbohydrate, protein, and fat. Alcohol and caffeine should be avoided, because they increase heat loss and water loss, respectively.

In conclusion, the body has two ways of internally generating heat: activity (exercise) and the metabolism of food. External heat sources include radiation from the sun (not dependable), fire, and warming huts. Understanding hypothermia combined with regular monitoring and good communication should help you catch it in the early stages should it occur in your group.

Afterdrop   The body's core temperature can actually decrease during rewarming, a phenomenon known as afterdrop. It is caused by blood vessels in the arms and legs dilating because the person is rewarming too quickly or externally. This dilation sends very cold, stagnant blood from the periphery to the core, further decreasing core temperature and potentially leading to death. Afterdrop can best be avoided by not rewarming the periphery. Rewarm the core only! Do not expose a severely hypothermic victim to extremes of heat.

Risk Management

Prevention and proper planning are crucial to managing risk and ensuring participants' physical and emotional safety. Solid preparation will help you lead safe, engaging activities. You need to be aware not only of the normal risks of outdoor winter activity, but also of the greater risks of dealing with traffic, other pedestrians, and the environment. No risk factor is completely avoidable, but by addressing safety considerations before and during the activity, you can take steps to protect yourself and your participants. To create a safe learning environment for all, develop a solid risk management plan that outlines ways to recognize, confront, and reduce risks. Following are the primary factors to consider in managing risk:

- Environment (e.g., weather, terrain, exposure)
- People involved (e.g., age, dress)
- Skill levels and experience of participants
- Leadership ability and experience of leaders in the activity and environment
- Materials (e.g., fires, stoves, sharp objects)

> ### *The Ice Man*
> Dutch daredevil Wim Hof, nicknamed the Ice Man, holds the world record for fastest half-marathon run barefoot on snow and ice. In 2007, Hof completed the half-marathon in two hours and 16 minutes in Oulu, Finland.

You must be familiar with participants' expectations and set boundaries for the participants in each session. These basics must be reviewed regularly. In dealing with a safety incident of any size, follow your safety plan. Concerns related to risk must be addressed immediately. You are responsible for ensuring that everyone in the group is responsible and engaged to ensure a safe and positive learning experience. The goal for each activity should be that both participants and leaders feel good about the experience.

For our purposes, we consider risk management in three phases:

- **Phase 1:** Planning and preparation (P&P) before the activity (creating a risk management plan)
- **Phase 2:** During the activity (begins when the first participant arrives and ends when the last participant leaves)
- **Phase 3:** Debriefing and evaluating after the activity to consider what was good and recommend any changes for the future

Be sure to build all organizational policies and procedures into each aspect and phase of your risk management plan. Recognizing that policies are intended as a guide, and not a prescription, does not give carte blanche immunity to the leader or organization in the event of a mishap. In the case of unforeseen discrepancies, acknowledge such as they arise; inform participants and your superiors as appropriate.

Phase 1: Before the Activity

We want people in our groups to enjoy winter, not to be turned off by another snowfall. This is one of the many reasons that ensuring their safety with proper planning is so crucial. Following are tasks that are integral to planning and preparing for winter activities:

- In the preprogram preparation, complete the discussion of objectives and assign P&P duties to each (e.g., activity program schedule and duties—Andrew; equipment prep and check—TA; preparation and collection of participant forms—Kevin).
- Assess the landscape and choose appropriate locations for activities.
- Attend to the paperwork: at-a-glance forms, medical forms, emergency safety plan, gear checks.
- Review the activities and check the materials and equipment.
- Ensure that all leaders have first aid training to match the nature and location of the activity. For activities in the wilderness, wilderness first aid is important; encourage as many leaders as possible to obtain higher levels of first aid.

Creating a risk management process can help you identify risks. Following are steps to guide you in this process:

- Mentally visualize each step in the activity or session.
- Ask yourself aloud, Are there any dangers?
- If you have coleaders, walk through or role-play the activity, making sure you do it step-by-step.
- Brainstorm with your leadership team and write down any possible harmful incidents that could occur during the activity.
- Prepare a written plan of action to deal with the most likely incidents.
- Perform this assessment for every activity you will be leading.
- Evaluate and reassess each activity on a regular basis, (e.g., after every session, season, or year).

Every program, activity, group, and participant has unique considerations in terms of risk. Moreover, all winter activities carry risks related to cold, snow, ice, and weather. This is why you must carefully consider all risks before every program or activity.

Medical Information

The generic medical information form in figure 2.3 provides basic health information you will need before making physical demands on an individual or a group. Having this information prior to meeting the group is helpful. Your program should have a structured information intake process to give the leadership team time to follow the P&P sequence. This includes ensuring that you complete all paperwork or forms required by your organization.

Route Planning

A route card documents your travel plan in terms of where you expect to be and when. This document, along with the at-a-glance form (see chapter 1), should be left with a dependable person (e.g., program administrator, park warden, principal, local police department, government official from a resource or environment department). If you and your group do not check in at the expected time, you have a record of your expected (approximate) location. This may seem like low technology, but a route card can be a very dependable tool, along with others addressed later in the book.

A sound practice is to break your excursion into thirds: one third of your time should be spent traveling; one third should be spent in maintenance mode (e.g., water in/water out, adding/removing layers, applying mole skin to hot spots that may become blisters if left untreated); and one third should be spent resting, relaxing, and playing (see figure 2.4). This is not appropriate for groups that meet for only an hour after school, however; most of their time should be spent engaged in the activity or game. Breaking extended day and overnight trips into thirds helps pace the session and prevents a bad case of get-there-itis.

The route card maps out your intended route of travel in addition to being a systematic method for planning and recording your route. It is useful for the following reasons:

- It encourages you to examine many important details of your trip such as direction, distance, time, terrain, and hazards. Such a close examination often discloses points overlooked in preliminary planning.
- It is a written record for use during your trip. If you are not proceeding at the calculated pace, you will know that you need to make changes.
- It is a written record to leave with the appropriate authorities along with an emergency safety plan form. These people will take the appropriate action if you do not return at the prearranged time. Of course, you must ensure that you follow the prescribed route (or one of the alternate escape routes you have recorded) so that in the event a search must be organized, it is directed to the right area. A properly completed route card enables emergency responders to find you and takes much of the guesswork out of their response.

FIGURE 2.3   Participant Medical Information Form

Name:_____   Male or female:_____

Date of birth:_____

Address: _____

Phone number: _____

Name and phone number of family physician: _____
_____

Health card or health insurance information: _____
_____

In case of emergency, notify (please provide name, address, and phone numbers):
_____
_____

Medical concerns (allergies, seizures, chronic conditions, etc.). Please be specific.
_____
_____

Medications	Dosage	Frequency

Have you had any recent injuries or illnesses? If yes, please explain: _____
_____
_____
_____

I hereby declare that all the information provided is correct and accurate to the best of my knowledge.

Signature: _____

Parent or caregiver signature: _____

Included in the route card are the following:

- **Leg.** This refers to the stage in your journey. Leg 4 would be the fourth stage.
- **6FGR.** An abbreviation of "six figure," 6FGR is the six-digit number that corresponds to the location on a map that has been divided into a grid. It is identified by the intersection of two lines: an x-axis, called the "easting," and a y-axis, called the "northing."

- - - - -CUT - - - - - - - - - CUT- - - - - - - -CUT - - - - - -CUT - - - - - - -CUT - - - - - - -

The following is for your information. PLEASE SAVE!

Outdoor pursuit:

Location: _____

_____

_____

Drop-off: _____

_____

Pickup: _____

_____

You may contact the [leader's name] at [organization number] if you have any questions regarding this outdoor pursuit.

The group leaders for this outdoor pursuit are:

_____

_____

_____

_____

These group leaders are experienced outdoor leaders and are appropriately certified to lead groups in the selected outdoor pursuit. The safety and well-being of the participants are our top priority.

Requirements

- Participants must have every item on the equipment list before the trip departure date.
- Participants must bring personal medications with their first aid kits.
- Participants must adhere to the safety contract, or they will be removed from the outdoor pursuit.
- Please read the detailed information letter and trip itinerary and must return the permission form.

- **Grid bearing.** This is the bearing taken off the map for that leg of the journey.
- **Magnetic bearing.** This is the grid bearing adjusted with the declination in your area. In the example in figure 2.4, a declination of 20 degrees has been added to the grid bearing.
- **ETT.** The estimated travel time for that leg of the journey.
- **Terrain description.** A description of the physical features of the terrain for that leg of the journey.

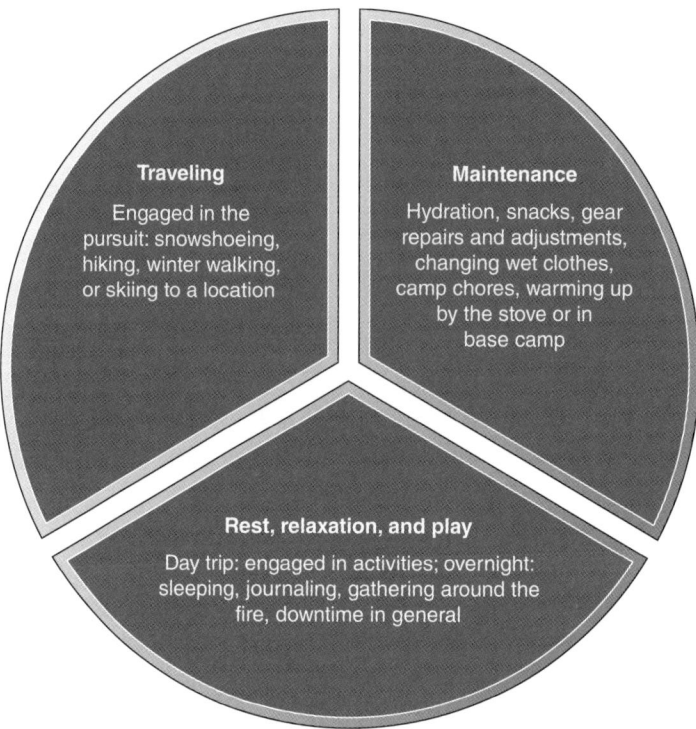

FIGURE 2.4　Break your excursion time into thirds.

A sample route card is shown in figure 2.5.

Activity Plan　The activity plan (see figure 2.6) lays out the activities of your program. For any length of trip, there may be spots along the way that are perfect for what you want to do with the group. To help keep focus, preventing the head-down, march-on syndrome ("What did you see along the way?" "Nothing"), break the leg up with things to do and notice, and keep this in balance with your thirds. For example, consider a hiding or camouflage activity in a forested section of your route. Or provide participants with a list of features to photograph along the route (e.g., a mature forest, a panoramic view from a hilltop, wildlife, any other local feature that encourages participants to engage with the landscape). Planning your activities in this way does not mean there will be no impromptu teachable moments; these happen too—if you are attuned to the environment and your group.

Emergency Safety Plan (ESP) Form　To maintain the highest level of safety during the program, you should complete an ESP form (see completed form in figure 2.7). This document travels with the main trip leader. A copy of the ESP along with the original route card outlining the trip should be left with the proper authorities such as the school principal. This documentation will also travel with the leaders and be attached to the plan book or activity logbook. Each ESP form will reflect the unique location, age of the participants, season of the year, and nature

FIGURE 2.5   Route Card

Name:_____   Date:_____

Activity:_____   Maps:_____

Leg number	Home 6FGR	Destination 6FGR	Grid bearing	Magnetic bearing	ETT	Terrain description
1	123 456	133 890	90 E	110 E	25 min	Rolling open field
2	133 890	143 890	340 N	360 N	20 min	Hilly forest trail

FIGURE 2.6   Activity Plan

Leg number	Activity location/ 6FGR	Name of activity	General description	Resources required	Modifications
1	123 456	Bird watch	Find as many bird cutouts as you can on the edge of the trail. 2-3 min	Bird cutouts in trees	Call out when you find one, or try to keep it secret and photograph them.
2	133 890	Comfort check	Rest stop 3-5 min Water in, water out Check for hot spots (start of blisters) and body temps, and adjust dress or layers.	Moleskin for hot spots	Buddy up for a roll call.

of the emergency. Before heading out with your group, be sure to review your ESP so that the information is fresh in your mind.

Phase 2: During the Activity

We always begin the trip by reviewing travel and play guidelines and clarifying our expectations. We try to keep this simple: no negative comments; no name-calling; lend a hand if needed; stick to the boundaries; if you're not sure, ask; play fair; and a few others. The point of guidelines is to build a safe community for all participants. Feel free to make your own.

Keeping communication respectful and open creates the trust needed in outdoor programs. Groups that function well can be given more choices in terms of activities and the type and duration of excursions. Moreover, participants in such

FIGURE 2.7 Emergency Safety Plan

Location	Monks Head, Antigonish, Nova Scotia
Group size	12 participants, 2 leaders
Trained first-aiders	2 WRFA* advanced, 1 WRFA basic
Leaders	TA, Andrew and Kevin
Leaders in training	N/A
Activities	• Instant activity: not me—YOU! (No tackling, pushing, grabbing clothing) • Three trees: tree identification (off main trail, stay in group; third of group with Kevin (blue), third with Andrew (red), third with TA (green) • Participants must always be in sight of their group leader.
Departure from school	Wednesday, February 10, 2016, 3:10 p.m.
Return to school	Wednesday, February 10, 2016, 4:45 p.m.
Safety considerations	• The emergency signal is three blasts of the whistle. • When the whistle is blown, all activities must immediately end and participants must stay with their leaders. • All participants must have whistles attached to their coats. • The buddy system (triads) will be enforced during field sessions. • Leaders will monitor participants for hydration and energy levels and signs and symptoms of frostbite. • Leaders will remind participants of special considerations for the terrain and safe behaviors: ascending and descending steep hills on snowshoes. • For minor problems that require an activity to end quickly but to not cause alarm, a code word will be decided on and practiced for the entire session (e.g., *plankton*). Once that word is called out, all activities end immediately, and participants return to their leaders. • No one may wander off; all participants must stay in their groups of three or four at all times. Anyone requiring special attention should speak to his or her leader.
Injury and evacuation procedure	1. If an accident occurs, the participant will be assessed on-site by the leader. 2. The leader will determine whether the session will end and the entire group return to base camp. 3. If a return is required, the group will follow the predetermined route (see map and designated quick trails). 4. The leaders will stay with the participants until all are picked up by their parents or caregivers. 5. All injuries, symptoms, and illnesses should be reported to a designated buddy, who will immediately inform a GO leader. 6. If evacuation is not possible because of the nature of the injury, the leaders will follow the established emergency procedures plan.

*WRFA = wilderness and remote first aid

groups experience substantial personal growth. To cultivate such a program environment, you need to ensure that participants are safe. In addition to the preceding guidelines, we remind our participants of the following safety points:

- The emergency signal is three blasts of the whistle. The whistles are to be used only for this purpose.
- The group must stay on the route unless an emergency results in an immediate evacuation.
- All participants must have a whistle.
- The buddy system is in place during the entire trip.
- All participants are responsible for carrying a ready-to-eat first meal and personal snacks.
- All participants are responsible for their own water.
- Group members may not deliberately engage in high-risk activity.
- At least one cell phone will be taken on the trip.

When an incident occurs, do not dismiss it as inconsequential. Address it with first aid procedures, and follow the next appropriate steps required for the well-being of the group. Your emergency safety plan (ESP) helps reduce risks simply by raising awareness in the group. Ultimately, though, you must decide whether the risk inherent in an activity is acceptable.

Use your ESP to determine the best course of action when a risky situation arises. To determine the severity of a risk, consider the following:

- Participants' emotional, mental, and physical state
- Participants' ability to perform skills
- Other program leaders' emotional, mental, and physical state
- State of the equipment and whether the gear is operational within the current environmental conditions
- Weather (Is it more challenging than the group can handle?)

Before making the decision to stop an activity, ask yourself these questions:

- Am I following the existing policies and rules that govern our GO program excursions?
- Does my instinct tell me not to continue?
- Can further risk be prevented, or will the risk persist during the activity?

The answers to these questions will help you make an informed decision so that you can answer yes to the question "Am I in the right place at the right time with the right group doing the right activity with the right equipment?" Figure 2.8 shows a simple in-field risk management decision tree to help you determine whether to continue with an activity, modify it, or end it because of safety concerns. Our position is as follows: If it does not feel right, or you are not sure, return

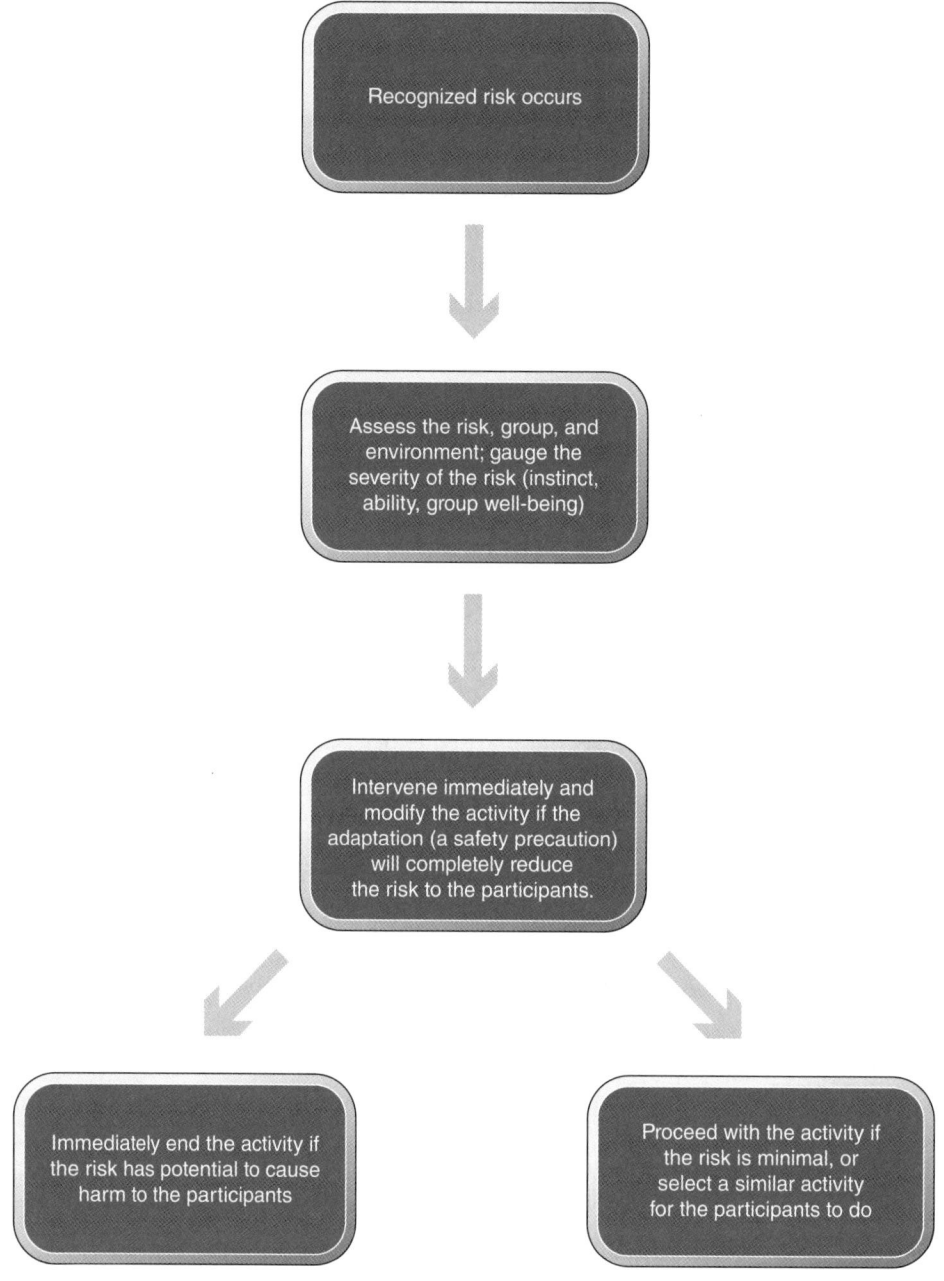

FIGURE 2.8 Risk management decision tree for field use.

to base camp. There is always an opportunity to reset, try something different, gain perspective, and learn from your experiences as you strive to create safe and positive learning opportunities. Finally, make sure to include all organizational policies and procedures in your risk management plan.

If an accident occurs, an assessment should occur on-site to determine whether evacuation is necessary. Here is an example of an ESP:

- If the injured person cannot be extracted from the site, a group of no fewer than three people will travel to the trailhead to notify the appropriate emergency personnel. The group will follow routes noted on the route card.
- The evacuation site will be the trailhead *[include 6FGR coordinates]*.
- The first person at an accident site will initiate first aid.
- Regardless of perceived significance, all injuries, symptoms, and illnesses will be reported through the buddy system.
- The trip leader has the right to cancel or end the trip based on current or pending weather conditions.
- The emergency bearing is *[provide bearing coordinates]*.

Phase 3: Debriefing

An essential component of any program is the debriefing following the program. The fact that safety is the primary concern in any program amplifies the need to reflect on current practices and debrief recent incidents. It may not be necessary to complete a formal review after each outing, but you should log reflection notes. Serious incidents require a review as soon as possible after an incident is resolved. Your organization should have regular reviews of your emergency and safety policies and procedures that should include the following:

- Review of all forms completed by others (participants, guardians, etc.)
- Review of all forms completed by leaders (to ensure they reflect your intent and your needs)
- Storage of all forms collected (not only for documentation value but also for future reference)
- Suitability of the environment to participants
- Participant engagement and procedural compliance
- Participant skill levels
- Leadership ability
- Equipment being used and how
- Groups' ability to stay within set parameters
- Groups' ability for self-governance
- Leader preparation
- Participant preparation
- What worked really well
- Limitations and what needs improving

Summary

Safety and risk management are essential considerations for any outdoor leader. Proper preparation includes safety and risk management as a means to reduce the human and environmental risks inherent in the activity and also to establish a system or protocol in the event of an incident.

Getting outside in winter has some specific risks related to the effects of cold on people and the environment. Assessing environmental conditions is important in helping participants and leaders dress and prepare appropriately for the range of environmental conditions the group can reasonably expect to encounter. For example, wind chill risk management would involve limiting exposure times in specific temperature ranges. Risks such as dehydration and hypothermia may occur in any season, but in winter such conditions may be less visible or may be accelerated or exacerbated by cold temperatures.

Applying sound risk management principles throughout the first two phases of activity (before and during activity) reduces the risk of the activity and provides predefined strategies or protocols to follow to address any issues that may occur. In the third activity phase (debriefing and postactivity assessment), positive practices are reinforced and shortcomings become learnings that may be applied in future.

Being prepared for the worst and being in a position to handle any risk management issue with confidence not only contributes to a safer experience but also nurtures a buoyant tone toward challenge within the group.

References

Boat Safe Kids. (1999). How to be a storm spotter. www.boatsafe.com/kids/weather1.htm

Doswell, C. (2001, December 21). Thunderstorms and camping safety. www.cimms.ou.edu/~doswell/tstm_camping_safety.html

Redmond, K., Foran, A., Dwyer, S. (2010). *Quality lesson plans for outdoor education*. Champaign, IL: Human Kinetics.

Wilderness survival skills for safe wilderness travel. (2007). How to predict weather using natural signs. www.wilderness-survival-skills.com/how-to-predict-weather.html

Chapter 3
Winter Gear and Clothing

When participants are comfortable, they can focus on the fun and any lessons you want to impart. On the other hand, when they're cold and wet, it's just about impossible to learn anything or have any kind of fun. There's no doubt about it—moving around in the snowy outdoors requires clothing that keeps people reliably dry and warm. This chapter addresses the clothing and gear people need for all levels of participation in winter outdoor activities, from the schoolyard to remote snowy trails (more specialized equipment is discussed in later chapters). We outline the important items you will need to bring on all excursions, and some of the equipment that opens up a wider world of winter activity for your program.

Basic Gear

Although people do need more gear and clothing when going outdoors in winter than they do in other seasons, they don't have to buy a lot of fancy, expensive winter clothes to stay comfortable. Following some basic layering principles can help anyone dress for the cold outdoors. When planning what to wear outdoors in cold weather, think in terms of the three Ws: wick, warm, and weather (wind and water).

• **Wick.** The base layer, which is worn next to the skin, is preferably made of wool or a synthetic material (i.e., not cotton). This fabric should resist absorbing sweat and wick it away from the body. We refer to this layer as hydrophobic (water hating); because of this property, it helps keep you feeling dry and, therefore, warm. Base layers come in various thicknesses: lightweight, midweight, and heavy weight. The temperature outside and the level of activity will influence your choice of base layer thickness. Colder, more sedate activities require a thicker base layer, whereas an activity such as Nordic skiing in warmer temperatures requires a lighter option.

- **Warm.** The clothing worn over the base layer is often called the insulation layer. Depending on the temperature and your level of activity, you may require one or more warm layers over your base layer and under your outer shell. Your warm layers should be made of wool, down, or synthetic materials such as polyester (i.e., fleece). You should not wear cotton clothing as an insulating layer because of the danger of hypothermia. Cotton is hydrophilic (water loving) and thus holds water, making you damp and cold.

- **Weather.** The last layer in the system, often called the shell layer, protects you from the weather (i.e., wind and water). It also provides an outer envelope that helps contain your body heat in the insulating layers. Ideally, the outer shell is made from material that is windproof, waterproof, and breathable. There is often a trade-off between breathability and waterproofness. For example, a material that is 100 percent waterproof is not very breathable, if at all. A highly breathable material is often not very waterproof. In cold, dry conditions, nonwaterproof (i.e., more breathable) materials are best because they allow sweat to evaporate, keeping you drier and warmer than waterproof gear can. In cold, dry winter environments, a tightly woven cotton canvas pullover can be an excellent option. Canvas provides a windproof barrier and is highly breathable, allowing the moisture to move away from the wicking layer, out through the warming layer, to the outer weather layer. As an outer shell, a mid-thigh-length canvas anorak with a fur-trimmed hood, over a warm layer, provides excellent comfort in high wind and cold. In cold, damp conditions, a breathable waterproof material such as Gortex or eVent is often the best choice for the outer shell.

> ### The First Latex Boots?
>
> The ancient Mayans made cuts in rubber trees to extract latex, which they used to coat their feet. The coating functioned like a waterproof boot!

The three Ws can also be used for making clothing choices for hands and feet as well. Start with a wicking layer—liner socks and gloves that wick away moisture and are made of wool or synthetic materials. Over these, layer warmer mittens or gloves, or socks, made of wool or polyester fleece for insulation. Finally, over this insulation, wear nylon or leather mitten or glove shells as your last hand layer and leather or rubber boots as your last foot layer.

Mittens are a much warmer choice than gloves because the fingers share a warm space, but gloves provide greater dexterity. Nylon is a good shell choice in wet or damp conditions and dries quickly. Leather works well in cold, dry conditions and lasts longer than nylon, but it takes a long time to dry. Gear should match the conditions as well as your activities. For example, activities that require high energy output, such as Nordic skiing, often generate lots of heat, so lighter gloves can be adequate. Whatever your choice, always pack extra gloves, mittens, and socks so you can change them if they get damp.

Leather is a good shell boot option, but there will be a maintenance consideration (i.e., keeping the leather waterproof. Rubber eliminates almost all of the waterproof concern, but it takes on cold. If the boot is poorly insulated, the result will be cold feet! A typical winter boot will work just fine for day programs and overnights, but for more advanced expeditions, you might want a more technical boot. Moccasins are a traditional winter foot covering. They are so warm, light, and comfortable that we call them winter sandals! They work best in dry and cold winter conditions.

Paul Kirtley, expert Bushcraft instructor, says that for winter activities, you should "Be bold; start cold." His direction is to start out a little underdressed and allow your body to heat up with activity to avoid overheating and sweating, thus saturating your layering system with moisture. Dampness and wet will lead to uncomfortable participants. Suggest that your participants start the excursion feeling slightly cool. If, after some activity, they are still chilled, stop and have them put on another layer from their backpacks and resume moving. Layering requires practice. Being comfortable outdoors in winter requires that we make constant adjustments as we warm up and cool down. Here is a suggested list of clothing and equipment for participants:

- Day pack with a capacity between 15 and 20 liters (915 to 1,220 cu in., a book-bag type of pack)
- Closed-cell foam mat for sitting or standing on (I provide "bum spots" for my class made from a full-length pad cut into squares large enough to sit on; students are required to sign them out.)
- Waterproof envelope to carry a field journal or activity sheets
- Headlamp or flashlight
- Personal first aid kit (with any required medications)
- Ski goggles to cover eyes (they do help!) on windy days
- Sunglasses
- Sunscreen
- Lip balm
- Water bottle
- Thermos (if possible) filled with hot water (saves time if a quick warm drink is needed)
- Snacks and lunch
- Rain gear
- Long underwear bottoms and tops (synthetic or wool)
- Heavy wool or synthetic pants covered with nylon wind pants or snow pants
- Light base layer (fleece or wool)
- Medium-weight sweater (fleece or wool)
- Heavyweight sweater (could be a pullover or jacket style)
- Windproof jacket (nylon shell or anorak)
- Standard winter coat or parka with a hood (down filled is nice)
- Warm wool or fleece hat (extra)
- Face mask, neck tube, or balaclava; wool scarf
- Wool mittens and mitten covers (extra)
- Wool socks (extra)

We expand on this general list in other chapters to include more specialized pieces of clothing and gear you may want to consider for winter camping or expeditions. But for now, this general layering introduction and suggested list is an excellent starting point for helping your participants stay comfortable and active outside in winter.

Wintertime Essentials for the Leader Pack

When you go beyond the schoolyard or recreation center boundary with a group in the winter, your leader pack will be a little heavier than it would be in summer. Don't fret too much, however, because we've got a great acronym to help you remember what to put in your pack: WINTERTIME! Here is the list of gear that should be in your backpack if you are going off-site with your group to nearby woods or farther afield to a more remote location.

- **W**ater and food
- **I**nsulation
- **N**avigation
- **T**echnology for communication
- **E**mergency first aid kit
- **R**epair kit
- **T**hings for sun protection
- **I**llumination
- **M**aterials for fire making
- **E**mergency shelter and shovel

Water and Food

As the leader, you should always carry extra water and food in case participants spill theirs, the weather changes, or the group moves slower than expected. Additionally, pack a method for purifying water in the field, such as a water filter, chemical disinfectant, or stove. To keep water from freezing during a winter outing, you can carry hot water in a thermos, use a commercially made water bottle insulator, make a water bottle insulator yourself, or put your water bottle in an extra wool sock. Whatever strategy you choose, keep your water bottle in the middle of your pack rather than hanging from the side if the temperature is much below freezing.

A quality thermos provides a supply of hot drinks through a daylong outing without having to light a stove. It's great for warming you or your participants from the inside out. Pack some hot chocolate, tea, or instant soup as well. Most people find warm water easier to drink during the winter, which helps with hydration. The amount each person needs to drink is individual, but planning on two liters (or quarts) per person per day is a good place to start. Plan for more if your group will be very active or climbing to high altitudes.

A sampling of leader pack items.
© Andrew Foran

Pack some extra food as well in case you are delayed in your return. Ideally, this food should be easy to eat (even if frozen), require no cooking, and keep well for long periods (so you can keep it in your leader pack over the whole season). Some possibilities are dried fruit, nuts, jerky, chocolate, candy, and granola.

Insulation

In wintertime, insulation is key. Just as you need to insulate your water bottles, you also need to insulate your body, including head, hands, and feet. It's a good idea to have extra insulation to offer participants in case they get cold or wet, so pack an extra fleece jacket, hat, mittens, and wool socks. Keep a supply of disposable hand and toe warmers in your pack in case a participant gets really cold hands or feet. Pack all of this into a waterproof pack liner bag or garbage bag to ensure that it stays dry. When you take a break or sit down on the snow, it's important to insulate yourself from the cold. Be willing to sit on your backpack, or bring a lightweight foam pad, known as a sit-upon, so you always have a warm spot to sit.

Navigation

Snow can cover the trail or your tracks in winter, so it's important to carry a topographic map of the area you are visiting and know how to use it. Laminate this map or place it in a protective case or plastic bag to protect it from snow or blustery weather. Along with your map, pack a compass. You may want to carry other navigational tools such as a global positioning system (GPS) unit, altimeter, guidebook, or route description, depending on how far you are venturing and the terrain you are traveling in.

Technology for Communication

Your choice of technology for communication depends on where you are traveling with your group. A cell phone helps with emergency communications; a smartphone in particular has lots of tools for navigation and apps for the outdoors (bird identification, avalanche advisories, etc.). If you are traveling with a large group, handheld radios for group leaders can be useful. If you are traveling in areas outside of cell phone coverage, you may want to consider carrying a satellite-based communication device such as a DeLorme inReach or Globalstar SPOT messaging system, a personal locator beacon (PLB), or a satellite phone.

Because winter temperatures can significantly reduce battery life in devices, carry your technology in a waterproof bag in a pocket near your body. The waterproof bag will keep the device from being harmed by your sweat as well as by snowy, wet conditions. If your device has a removable battery, you can keep just the battery in an inner pocket. Bring extra batteries, a portable charger, or both.

Emergency First Aid Kit

It's always best to take the steps necessary to avoid injury or sickness, but the unexpected can happen. For this reason, you should always carry and know how to use a first aid kit. The size of your kit will depend on where you are headed and how far you will be from medical care. At a minimum, your kit should contain protective gloves, small adhesive bandages, gauze pads of various sizes, roller gauze, adhesive tape, scissors, a triangular bandage, a SAM splint, soap, wound cleanser, antibiotic ointment, paper, and pencil. Carry your first aid kit in a waterproof container or bag.

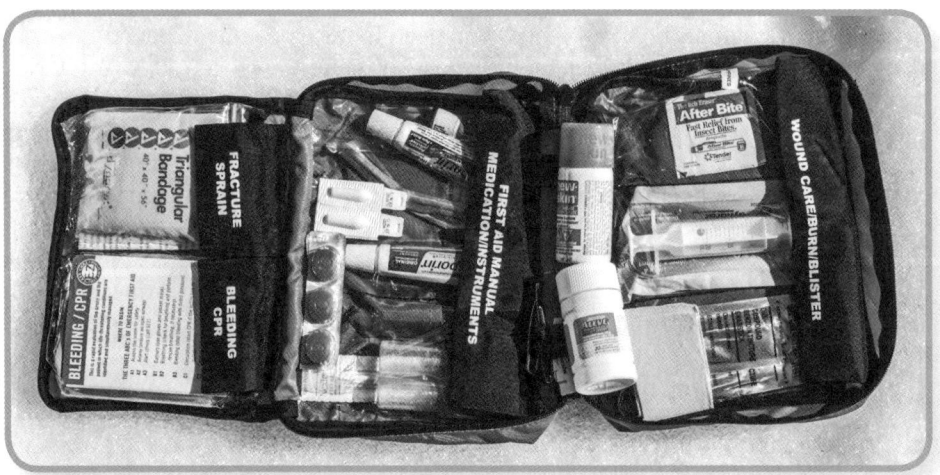

Emergency first aid kit.
© Kevin Redmond

Repair Kits

Knives are useful for outdoor leaders for first aid, food preparation, gear repair, and more. Often, a knife is part of a multitool that includes pliers, a screwdriver, an awl, and scissors, making it easy to carry all the tools you might need to repair your stove, skis, or snowshoes. Check your ski and snowshoe bindings to make sure your multitool has the size and kinds of implements you need to adjust or repair them. Some other useful items to keep in your repair kit are shoelaces, safety pins, needle and thread, wire, duct tape, nylon fabric repair tape, cable ties, plastic buckles, a parachute cord, and spare parts for equipment such as a stove, snowshoes, and skis.

Some leaders like to prepare separate repair kits for each category of gear. For example, a ski-specific repair kit could contain items such as five-minute epoxy, a spare ski pole basket, a pole splint, hose clamps for pole repair, and extra binding parts such as screws, bolts, and cables. Because stove parts are specific to each brand and model of stove, a repair kit needs to be built for each stove; it should include specific tools and parts as well as lubricating oil for the pump leather (if necessary; some stoves don't have pumps).

Things for Sun Protection

With snow on the ground, you and your group will be exposed to the sun twice: from the sky and reflected from the snow. Dark sunglasses are critical when outside in the winter. Carry a spare pair in case one breaks. Given the double exposure to the sun, it's important to use sunscreen on lips and skin. Everyone should reapply both often because it is very easy to wipe it off your nose and lips accidently. Snow blindness and sunburned lips are no fun. Prevention is key.

Illumination

Winter days are short. Even if you plan to return before dark, it is essential to carry a headlamp or flashlight, just in case you get caught out. Pack extra batteries and a spare bulb as well. Also, pack an extra light source in case one of your participants forgets to bring one.

Materials for Fire Making

If you are traveling beyond your neighborhood or schoolyard, you should have materials to start and sustain a fire. Carry your fire kit in a waterproof container or bag. It should contain two butane lighters, waterproof matches, candle stubs or tea lights, homemade or commercial fire starters, and dry tinder. Fire starters or dry tinder are indispensable for igniting wet winter wood quickly to make a campfire. It is also advisable to carry a backpacking stove and cooking pot as an additional source of emergency heat and water.

Emergency Shelter and Shovel

When packing wintertime essentials, the question in your mind should always be What if? Packing an emergency shelter or tarp as well as a shovel will help you manage a what-if. An emergency shelter commonly used in the United Kingdom is the bothy bag. This lightweight nylon bag is like a parachute that you hold over the group and then sit down on (the edges), quickly forming an immediate barrier from cold or wet weather. Once the group is in the bothy, the temperature inside will rise. Sitting on backpacks or foam pads in a bothy bag, the group can wait out a squall, have lunch, or administer first aid to an injured or hypothermic participant while keeping warm and dry. Bothy bags are available in various sizes to accommodate 2 to 20 people. Large plastic contractor garbage bags are also handy to pack as individual emergency tarps.

A snow shovel is a very handy tool for the winter leader to carry. If you are traveling in avalanche terrain, a shovel for each person in the group is mandatory. Digging with a shovel is much more efficient than digging with your hands. A variety of commercially available backcountry shovels are light and compact enough to fit inside a backpack or attach to the outside of one. You can tie a piece of cord or webbing to the handle and blade of the shovel so you can sling it over your shoulder if you are not wearing a pack. Shovels are great for digging out a fire pit, digging a test pit to check snow conditions, or making a snow shelter.

Figure 3.1 shows a complete checklist for leader gear.

Winter Travel Gear

With your backpack filled with wintertime essentials, it's time to choose the way you will travel through the snow. Depending on the amount of snow, you may be able to travel over packed trails wearing only winter boots. If the snow is deeper, you may need snowshoes; if you want to travel farther, Nordic skis may be your answer. If you have significant supplies to take along, you may want to consider using a sled to move your gear. The following sections describe in detail your options for sleds, snowshoes, and Nordic ski gear.

Pulks, Toboggans, and Sleds

Once you have added program materials, supplies, snacks, props for games, and so forth, you may decide that you need a snow transport system in addition to a backpack. The three primary choices are a basic sled, a toboggan, and a pulk. A basic sled with a rope is great for moving gear and supplies across a nearby field or snow-covered parking lot for on-site programming. It frees you from the task of carrying so you can avoid dropping gear and stumbling all the way to your destination.

A toboggan can carry an amazing amount of gear, but this hauling option is limited to fairly open trails because of its length. If you are traversing hilly terrain, you will need someone holding a line tied to the back of the toboggan, which is called a brake line. On descents, the person holding the brake line keeps the toboggan from chasing you down the hill. The toboggan can be a good choice for winter trekking (see chapter 9).

Once a Toboggan, Always a Toboggan

Toboggan design has changed very little since the first ones were made by First Nations cultures using whalebone, birch, and tamarack. Today's toboggan maintains the curve of the first design and is made of seven boards (usually ash or maple) about two inches wide.

FIGURE 3.1   WINTERTIME leader gear checklist.

Water and Food

- ○ Extra water
- ○ Water bottle insulator
- ○ Thermos
- ○ Hot chocolate, tea, or instant soup
- ○ Water purification filter or chemical disinfectant
- ○ Extra food (dried fruit, nuts, jerky, chocolate, candy, and granola)

Insulation

- ○ Extra fleece jacket
- ○ Extra knit hat
- ○ Extra mittens
- ○ Extra wool socks.
- ○ Disposable hand and toe warmers
- ○ Lightweight foam pad
- ○ Waterproof bag

Navigation

- ○ Topographic map
- ○ Compass
- ○ GPS unit
- ○ Altimeter
- ○ Guidebook
- ○ Route description

Technology for Communication

- ○ Cell phone
- ○ Handheld radios for leaders (large group)
- ○ Satellite-based communication (inReach, SPOT, PLB, satellite phone)
- ○ Waterproof case or bag
- ○ Extra battery or charging system for tech gadgets

Emergency First Aid Kit

- ○ Protective gloves
- ○ Small adhesive bandages
- ○ Gauze pads of various sizes
- ○ Roller gauze
- ○ Adhesive tape
- ○ Scissors
- ○ Triangular bandage
- ○ SAM splint
- ○ Soap
- ○ Wound cleanser
- ○ Antibiotic ointment
- ○ Paper
- ○ Pencil
- ○ Waterproof container or bag

Repair Kit

- ○ Knife
- ○ Screwdriver
- ○ Awl
- ○ Scissors
- ○ Shoelaces
- ○ Safety pins
- ○ Needle and thread
- ○ Wire
- ○ Duct tape
- ○ Nylon fabric repair tape
- ○ Cable ties
- ○ Plastic buckles
- ○ Parachute cord
- ○ Spare parts for equipment (stove, snowshoes, skis, etc.)

Things for Sun Protection

- ○ Sunglasses
- ○ Spare pair of sunglasses
- ○ Sunscreen
- ○ Lip balm

(continued)

FIGURE 3.1 *(continued)*

Illumination

- ⭘ Headlamp or flashlight
- ⭘ Spare headlamp or flashlight
- ⭘ Extra batteries
- ⭘ Spare bulb

Materials for Fire Making

- ⭘ Butane lighters (two)
- ⭘ Waterproof matches
- ⭘ Candle stubs or tea lights
- ⭘ Homemade or commercial fire starters

- ⭘ Dry tinder
- ⭘ Backpacking stove and cooking pot

Emergency Shelter and Shovel

- ⭘ Emergency shelter or tarp, or bothy bag
- ⭘ Large plastic contractor garbage bags (three)
- ⭘ Shovel (lightweight and collapsible)

A pulk is a sled with a harness system that attaches you to the sled via two fixed rods called traces. You will be surprised at how much you can stash and haul in a pulk (the snow removes a lot of the friction while hauling). The fixed traces prevent the sled from chasing you and banging the backs of your legs on downhills (which happens if you use a sled with a rope). Because a pulk travels very well off trail and through trees, it is the best choice if you are leaving the beaten path for the day or for an extended expedition.

Snowshoe Styles and Sizing

Snowshoeing is a great way to travel in winter landscapes. A fleet of snowshoes is much less expensive than a fleet of Nordic skis. Moreover, snowshoes are easier to learn to use than Nordic skis are, and they allow you to travel on many kinds of snow-covered terrain efficiently.

Snowshoes provide flotation on the snow by spreading your weight evenly over a large, flat surface area. This allows you to hike, climb hills, and even run over the snow. Traditionally, snowshoes were wooden frames with decking made of rawhide. Now, most snowshoes have aluminum or composite frames and synthetic decking. The snowshoe surface area needed to provide adequate flotation depends on your weight and the type of terrain and snow you are traveling over. Generally, the heavier the person or the more powdery the snow, the more snowshoe surface area is required. Although your weight provides some traction by pushing your snowshoes into the snow, many snowshoes feature serrated rails and toe crampons underfoot for greater grip and traction. As well, many snowshoes feature a V-shaped crampon under the heel. It provides traction on descents by filling with snow to slow you down. Because smaller snowshoes are generally easier to use than larger ones, aim to get the smallest size that will support your weight (or the weight of your participants) based on the snow conditions and kinds of terrain you will likely encounter.

Snowshoe bindings often consisting of nylon or rubber straps that wrap around the foot and heel, securing boots to the snowshoes. The two main types are floating and fixed. Floating bindings pivot under the balls of the feet, allowing you to walk naturally and climb hills. As you step, the tail of the snowshoe falls away, both reducing fatigue and shedding snow. This type of binding also makes it easy to make kick steps into steep slopes. Because the tail falls away in floating bindings, backing up or climbing over obstacles can be awkward. As the name suggests, fixed bindings remain attached at the heel, thereby bringing the snowshoe tails up with each step. This makes backing up and stepping over obstacles much easier. However, fixed bindings tend to kick snow onto the backs of your legs, necessitating the wearing of snow pants to stay dry.

Types of Snowshoes   Snowshoes fall into three categories that match the type of terrain for which they are best suited: beginner, intermediate, and advanced. Beginner snowshoes are designed for flat to rolling terrain. They are the least expensive and are ideal for groomed trail areas. Beginner snowshoes feature bindings that are easy to attach and adjust as well as moderate traction systems. Children and youth snowshoes often fit into the beginner category, and they have bindings that adjust to smaller boots. Like adult snowshoes, they are sized by the weight of the wearer. Each snowshoe manufacturer provides a chart that lists suggested sizes for body weights.

Some adult-sized snowshoes have bindings that can be made small enough to fit the boots of older children (ages 10 and up). These may be a good choice for programs that have both older children and adults. You may be able to negotiate a discount for a volume purchase of a class set. Also, grant programs are available to assist in the purchase of a fleet of snowshoes. Some municipalities and outdoor centers have snowshoes available for rent for an occasional outing.

Intermediate snowshoes are a step up from entry level and are designed to handle rolling to steep terrain. They can be used off groomed trails and are suitable for all but very steep or icy conditions. They have more aggressive traction features and more durable bindings.

Advanced snowshoes are for very icy and steep terrain, often found in mountain regions. These snowshoes are designed for mountaineers and are made with climbing-like crampon systems, rugged bindings, and the ability to add flotation tails when carrying a heavy load. Advanced snowshoes often have heel lifts, wire bails that can be flipped up to raise the foot and relieve calf strain on steep uphill sections.

Poles for Snowshoeing   It's possible to snowshoe without poles, but they make it easier for beginners to move over unpredictable terrain. You can use alpine, Nordic, or trekking poles. Size the poles so that the arms are at a 90 degree angle when holding the handgrip. Adjustable poles can be handy for fitting groups of various sizes. Ideally, poles for snowshoeing should have big baskets so they don't sink far into the snow, providing a more stable platform for balance.

Nordic Ski Styles and Sizing

Nordic skiing encompasses several styles, from touring on groomed ski tracks to racing to gliding through deep backcountry snow to skate skiing. In Nordic skiing, the skier's heel is always free (i.e., not connected to the ski), and the skier moves forward using either a striding motion (often called classic) or a side-to-side skating motion. This section covers Nordic ski gear selection and sizing for both classic and skate skiing.

There are four main types of Nordic skis:

- **Touring skis** are for use on groomed tracks and are generally lightweight, long, and narrow. This makes them fast and efficient. Many outdoor programs choose touring skis for their first fleet of skis.

- **Race skis** are similar to touring skis, but they're built for faster, more aggressive skiing. Because race skis are stiffer than touring skis, they are less forgiving and require better technique. Race skis would most likely be chosen by programs that want to develop a ski-racing program. Touring skis are the best choice when starting a program.

- Metal-edge touring skis are sometimes called **backcountry skis**. They are for skiing off-trail or on steeper terrain. They are typically shorter than touring skis for better maneuverability and wider for more stability and flotation in deeper snow. Backcountry skis often have metal edges for easier turning and better grip in icy conditions. As a result, they are heavier than touring skis but more suitable for off-trail terrain.

- **Skate skis** are used solely for skate skiing. They tend to be shorter, lighter, stiffer, and narrower than touring skis.

Touring skis and boots in action.
© Kevin Redmond

Ski Length   In most cases, body weight is more of a factor than height in determining ski length. Many ski manufacturers provide a skier weight range for each length of ski they sell. Shorter skis are slower but easier to handle for beginner skiers. In general, backcountry and skate skis are sized between 10 and 15 centimeters shorter than touring skis.

Ski Camber   Camber refers to the upward curve, or bow, in the middle of a ski. If you lay a ski flat on the ground, you can see its camber by noticing how much light is visible underneath the center of the ski. Camber affects both the flex and strength of a ski. Most touring skis have a double camber. When both skis are equally weighted (i.e., when gliding), the ski's grip zone remains raised off the snow to allow the ski to glide. When only one ski is weighted, the arch is completely flattened against the snow so that the ski grips the snow and gives traction for the skier's kick forward.

Camber is the reason body weight is more important than height in determining the correct ski length. The paper test is used to see if the skis' camber is correct for a skier. When the skier distributes body weight between the skis equally, a piece of paper should pass under the center of the ski easily. When the skier puts weight on only one ski, the paper should be trapped underfoot.

Skate skis are designed with a single camber. They have a gentler arch from the tip of the ski to the tail. This flatter profile allows skate skiers to push off the skis' edges more efficiently than they could on double-camber touring skis.

Ski Bases: Waxless and Waxable   In classic style, skis need to grip the snow to enable the skier to kick and then glide on flat terrain and to be able to climb hills. This grip can be achieved in two ways:

- **Waxless:** The kick zone has a mechanical grip pattern cut into it.
- **Waxable:** Grip wax is applied to the kick zone of the ski.

Waxless skis are so called because they don't rely on grip wax for traction; rather, they have a textured pattern in the kick zone that grips the snow. They are often chosen for institutional settings because of their ease of use and ability to provide

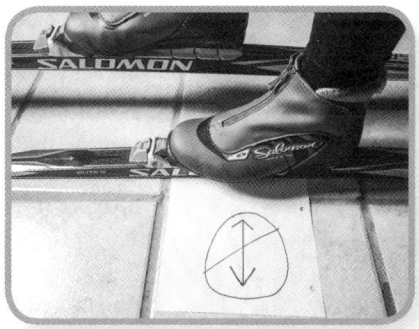

When the weight is equally distributed on both skis, you can slide the paper in and out under the front of the skis bindings.
© Kevin Redmond

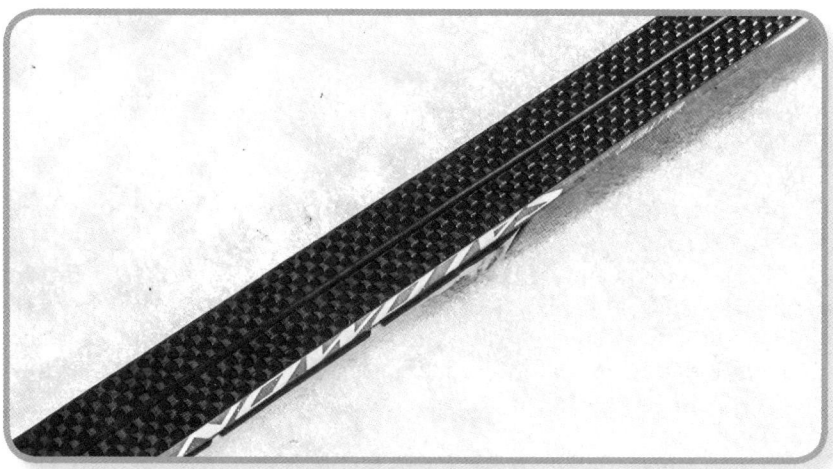

Bottom surface of a waxless ski.
© Kevin Redmond

grip in a variety of snow conditions. Despite their name, waxless skis require glide wax on the tips and tails to facilitate slipping over the snow when gliding.

Waxable skis require the application of grip wax on the kick zone for traction. The grip wax is chosen to match the snow's condition and temperature. This process is more time-consuming, but the benefit is that waxable skis glide better than waxless skis do. They also require glide wax on the tips and tails.

The edges of skate skis, rather than the bases, provide traction and forward momentum. As a result, skate skis are waxed for glide only.

Nordic Ski Boots

The ski boot is the connection between the skier's foot and the ski, so it must fit well. Nordic ski boots are designed to match each style of skiing. When trying on boots, start by wearing the socks you intend to ski in and try a boot that is the same size as your shoes. A well-fitting boot is comfortable, not too tight, and holds your feet solidly in place. You may need to size up or down, depending on the boot, to get this fit. Comfort is the number one priority when sizing ski boots.

Boots for touring offer a combination of flexibility for striding and torsional rigidity for turning and stopping. They are usually well insulated to keep feet warm. Boots for race classic skiing are lighter weight than touring boots, have lower cuffs, and are typically not as insulated. Boots for backcountry skis are higher cut, heavier, warmer, and stiffer to provide greater support for turning in deeper snow. Skate boots are higher cut than touring boots to offer more ankle support, and they have stiffer soles to minimize flex. Some programs choose "combi" boots that can be used for both classic and skate skiing.

Nordic Ski Bindings

When buying their first set of Nordic skis, most people choose their ski boots first; the boots' soles then dictate the bindings that will connect the boots to the skis.

Classic ski boot and bindings (*a*) and skate ski boot and bindings (*b*).
© Kevin Redmond

For example, boots with a New Nordic Norm (NNN) sole fit only NNN bindings. Once skiers gain more experience and begin to have preferences, they may choose a particular binding system and get boots that match.

Most manufacturers make one version of their binding systems for classic skiing and another for skate skiing. For example, there is a Salomon Pilot binding for classic skiing and another for skate skiing. You also need to choose between automatic and manual models of bindings. With automatic bindings, you can step right into them and usually release them with your ski pole. With manual bindings, you must reach down to lock your boots to the bindings or to release them.

The NNN binding system can be used for both classic and skating skiing styles. NNN bindings feature a catch in the binding that hooks onto a bar in the toe of the boot. This catch, which acts like a door hinge, along with a rubber bumper on the binding, allows forward flex and helps to lift the tail of the ski during the kick-and-glide motion of classic skiing and during the recovery motion of skate skiing. The backcountry variation (NNN BC) is wider, thicker, and more durable, and fits only NNN BC boots.

The Salomon Nordic System (SNS) binding system has two variations: SNS Profil and SNS Pilot. The SNS Profil bindings feature a single-rail design on the binding plate that matches a groove in the boot sole. It has a bar-and-catch system that is slightly narrower than that of the NNN system, thereby making the boots and bindings incompatible with NNN boots and bindings. SNS Pilot bindings have a binding rail similar to that on the Profil bindings, but instead of a single metal rod at the toe, Pilot boots use two metal rods to click into two slots in the binding. This additional connection creates increased stability and control during the kick motion, but results in some incompatibility; SNS Profil boots cannot fit into Pilot bindings, but SNS Pilot boots can fit into most Profil bindings. There are SNS Profil and SNS Pilot binding versions for both classic and skate skiing styles.

The 75-millimeter, or three-pin, binding is a traditional binding used primarily now for backcountry skis. The binding has three pins that hook into three holes in the front of the boot and a bail that locks the toe of the boot down to the ski. Although this binding offers a solid connection to the ski and is easily repairable in the field, it can be more cumbersome to attach into and out of than other systems are. The three-pin system can be used on touring skis as well, but does not perform well as a skate binding.

Nordic Ski Poles

As with skis, boots, and bindings, Nordic ski poles are designed for the style of skiing. Ski poles vary greatly in price based on material and strap system. Ski poles are made of bamboo, aluminum, fiberglass, and carbon fiber. More expensive poles are lighter and stiffer, and they offer better wrist strap systems.

Poles for classic touring on groomed trails should reach from the ground to the armpit, roughly 80 to 85 percent of your height. They typically have small baskets because they are used on packed snow. Poles for classic race skiing are similar to touring poles, but they are constructed of lighter, higher-quality materials. They are sized a few centimeters longer than a touring pole (i.e., midway between the armpit and the top of the shoulder).

Backcountry touring poles are heavier and more durable than regular touring poles. They have larger baskets so they sink less in deeper snow. Backcountry poles are often adjustable, so their length can be changed for ascending, descending, and traversing. This adjustability reduces their stiffness somewhat but makes sizing them very simple.

Skate poles are the longest of any of the styles. They need to be long enough to allow skiers to use all of the major muscle groups to propel them forward. As a general rule, skating poles should reach from the ground to somewhere between the chin and nose—about 90 percent of the skier's height. Skate poles are exposed to considerable force, so they must be stiff and durable. They usually have specially designed handgrips and wrist straps as well as asymmetrical baskets to make the skating technique comfortable and efficient.

As with snowshoes, there is often a discount for a volume purchase of a class set of Nordic skis. Package prices for buying the boots, skis, bindings, and poles together at the same time are often available. Grant programs you can apply to may help with the purchase of a fleet of Nordic skis. For initial outings with your group, a local outdoor center or municipality may have Nordic skis available for rent.

Summary

With wintertime essentials packed and your method of travel chosen, it's time to get outside. The following chapters are filled with heaps of activities to inspire you to go outside and enjoy the snowy joys of winter.

Snow Games and
Other Activities
Part II

Chapter 4
Icebreakers

Icebreakers, activities to help participants get to know each other and start to have fun, are key tools in any leader's toolbox. They should be fun, fast, and easy to do on the go. Icebreakers can play a double role in the winter environment because they can quickly warm up participants who have been inactive for a bit and are starting to get cold. In this case, they can literally break the ice!

Icebreakers get participants moving and interacting with each other, and can be a great bridge to the activities that follow. Some key points to remember when creating icebreakers in winter are covered by the acronym SNOWFLAKE.

- **S**now means slippery surfaces
- **N**ew activities often
- **O**utdoors is awesome
- **W**eave a story
- **F**un and flexible
- **L**ow prop requirements
- **A**lways active
- **K**now your group
- **E**nthusiastic participation that builds over time

Let's explore each of these a bit further.

- **Snow means slippery surfaces.** When choosing icebreakers, keep surfaces in mind. Some activities might need to occur at walking speed because of slippery surfaces caused by snow or ice.
- **New activities often.** Be prepared with several icebreaker activities so that you can change them frequently based on changing surface conditions; weather; or participants' attention span, body temperatures, focus, or abilities.

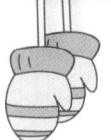

> ### Unique as a Snowflake?
>
> You have probably heard it said that no two snowflakes are alike. But in 1988 scientist Nancy Knight discovered two identical snowflakes while studying snow crystals from a storm in Wisconsin using a microscope!

- **Outdoors is awesome.** Don't be afraid to adapt beloved indoor icebreakers to the outdoors, or summer icebreakers to the winter.

- **Weave a story.** In addition to the many activities presented in this chapter, many common icebreakers can be changed into winter ones by weaving a story that captures some of the unique features of winter. Challenge yourself to find some new icebreakers to use rather than always going with your tried-and-trues.

- **Fun and flexible.** One of the main goals of icebreakers is fun. Keep your icebreaker agenda flexible so you can adjust your plan on the go. You may want to change the guidelines to suit your group or the weather. One group may be able to use snowballs, whereas another might need softer throwables. Remember that although icebreakers can help participants learn each other's names and break down barriers in the group, the number one purpose of an icebreaker is for the group to have fun.

- **Low prop requirements.** Given the propensity of snow to hide equipment, consider icebreakers with low prop requirements. Choose brightly colored, fun props if possible, and steer clear of white ones that will blend in with the snow.

- **Always active.** In winter, physical activity is often critical to remaining warm and happy. Keep instructions for icebreakers short and sweet to keep your group moving. Plan a few extra icebreakers that you can insert into a lesson plan to warm up participants if you find that you're talking too much and your group is getting cold.

- **Know your group.** Before deciding which icebreakers to use, check your group's vital signs: age, experience level, stage of group development, readiness for the weather, hunger, thirst, sense of humor, and so on. Try to keep in mind the five Gs of activity planning as well: goal, group, gear, guidelines, and gain.

- **Enthusiastic participation that builds over time.** When planning and sequencing your icebreakers, start slow and build intensity over time. It's often good to start with icebreakers that have simple guidelines, no props, and limited physical contact, and then progressively add activities that require more movement, physical contact, and complex instructions. Be an enthusiastic participant yourself and model the kind of participation you wish to see in your group.

Five Gs of Activity Planning

We introduced you to the five Gs of planning in chapter 1. Now that you are ready to jump into the planning of winter icebreakers, here is a quick checklist to use with yourself, your coleaders, and even your group.

Goal

- What are the overall goals for your program? Your outing? Your ice-breakers?
- What do you want your participants to learn and experience?
- Have the goals changed? If so, what else needs to change?

Group

- What is the experience and skill level of your group?
- How old are your participants?
- How well do they know each other?
- What is the group's stage of development?
- Do your participants have proper clothing and equipment for the weather?
- Are your participants warm enough?
- Are your participants hungry or thirsty?

Gear

- What outdoor gear do you need for the icebreakers you have planned?
- Is there any special gear that you have to bring along, or can you modify gear that you are already bringing?
- What props (if any) do you need to lead the icebreakers?
- What clothing or equipment do participants need?

Guidelines

- What guidelines and instructions will you use to frame the activities?
- Which teaching cues will you use?
- How will you set up activities in the snow?
- Do you need to adapt any of the activities because of weather or surface conditions?
- What safety and risk management concerns will you be watching for during the activity?
- What are your terrain needs?

Gain

- How will you make connections to key winter concepts?
- How will participants reflect on what they have learned during the activities?
- How will you process the experience with the group?
- How can you bridge participant gains to the goals of the activities?

Keep your icebreakers short and sweet, and make sure they keep your participants active!
© Andrew Foran

Activities

This section presents icebreakers and cooperative and team-building activities that can be used outside in winter. These activities can be used as part of a larger lesson or activity or combined to make a full lesson. Most take 5 to 15 minutes, but some last longer (up to 45 minutes). Equipment for these activities can be modified and adapted to meet the unique circumstances of your program and location.

Blizzard

Blizzard is a winter adaptation of the much-loved group juggle.

Age or Grade Level

Any age or grade level

Number of Participants

Any number of participants

Equipment

Snowballs or soft throwables (one per person)

Setup

Choose a level playing area.

How to Lead

- Form the group into circles of 10 to 12 participants.
- Each circle should have a leader who will help the group start their blizzard.
- Help the group establish a toss sequence to use throughout the activity (each person throws and catches once in the sequence). This is usually done by tossing a snowball underhanded across the circle until each group member has had a chance to both catch and throw it.
- The goal is for the group to create a blizzard by keeping as many snowballs in the air as possible using the sequence established in the first round.
- You can add a snowball into the blizzard at regular intervals as participants master throwing and catching the ones they have (e.g., once the group is comfortable with three snowballs, you can add a fourth, then a fifth, and so on).
- The usual maximum is one fewer snowball than the number of participants (e.g., nine snowballs in the air for 10 participants).

Variations

- Blizzard can be played with soft throwables instead of snowballs.
- Use extra winter hats or mittens rolled into balls as props.

Safety Consideration

If snow conditions do not allow for the formation of snowballs, or if snowballs would be too hard or icy, risking injury with a misthrow, use other throwables.

Blizzard Forecast

Blizzard can be progressed into a name game version, blizzard forecast, by having participants call each other by name before tossing the snowball as well as thanking those who pass them snowballs. For example, Participant 1: "Hey, Frosty, here's a snowball." Participant 2: "Thanks, Snowy Owl, for that great toss." You can also progress this activity further by asking participants to make sounds when tossing and catching snowballs. This often results in a cacophony of sights and sounds as snowballs are tossed amid much whirring, clicking, and swooshing. Participants could also be asked to make the sounds of winter-active wildlife or birds to tie the icebreaker even more strongly to the winter environment.

Age or Grade Level

Any age or grade level

Snowball Fight!

The biggest snowball fight ever took place in Seattle in 2013. This fundraiser event for the Boys and Girls Clubs of Seattle included 5,834 participants!

Number of Participants

Any number of participants

Equipment

Snowballs or soft throwables (one per person)

Setup

Choose a level playing area.

How to Lead

- Form the group into circles of 10 to 12 participants.
- Each circle should have a leader who will help the group start their blizzard.
- Have everyone in each circle say his or her name aloud.
- Help the group establish a toss sequence to use throughout the activity (each person throws and catches once in the sequence).
- As participants toss snowballs across the circle, they call out the names of the people to whom they are tossing.
- The receivers, in turn, thank the throwers for the toss.
- The goal is for the group to create a blizzard forecast by keeping as many snowballs and names flying through the air as possible using the sequence established in the first round.
- You can add a snowball to the blizzard at regular intervals as participants master throwing and catching the ones they have (e.g., once the group is comfortable with three snowballs, you can add a fourth, then a fifth, and so on).
- The usual maximum is one fewer snowball than the number of participants (e.g., nine snowballs in the air for 10 participants).

Variations

- Blizzard forecast can be played with soft throwables instead of snowballs.
- Use extra winter hats or mittens rolled into balls as props.
- In place of calling out names, participants can make two sounds, one as they toss and one as they receive. These can be silly sounds to act as a deinhibitizer. These sounds could also be winter-themed sounds (such as those made by active winter birds or animals) to introduce winter adaptations.

Safety Consideration

If snow conditions do not allow for the formation of snowballs, or if snowballs would be too hard or icy, risking injury with a misthrow, use other throwables.

Sinter Snowball Tag

When snow crystals lose their points, they sometimes freeze into larger crystals through a process called sintering. When we build snow shelters such as quinzhees, we use our shovels to compact the snow to allow sintering to occur before we dig out our living area. Sinter snowball tag is a fun, energetic tag game in which participants group together into various-sized clumps based on your instructions.

Age or Grade Level

Any age or grade level

Number of Participants

Any number of participants

Equipment

None

Setup

Choose a level playing area, and set boundaries for play depending on the group size.

How to Lead

- Based on surface conditions, decide whether the game will be played at walking, jogging, or running speed.
- Have participants spread out until they are standing at least 5 feet (1.5 m) apart (when they spread out their arms, they should not touch anyone else's arms).
- Explain that the goal is to form a clump (sinter) of people with the same number as you call out.
- Players must join hands or perform a group hug to sinter their small groups together. For example, if you call out "Sinter snowball seven," the large group breaks up into smaller clumps of seven.
- While this is occurring, try to tag players (i.e., snow crystals) who are still on the loose.
- The round ends when you tag someone or after about 30 seconds.
- A tagged player becomes the new leader and calls out the next sinter snowball number.

Variation

Sinter snowball tag can be played on snowshoes or skis as a warm-up or to practice changing direction in an active, engaging way.

Safety Consideration

Based on surface conditions, decide whether the game will be played at walking, jogging, or running speed.

Super Sinter Tag

Super sinter tag is a progression of sinter snowball tag as well as a winter adaptation of blob tag. Once the group understands the concept of sintering, this is a fun way to experience it.

Age or Grade Level

Any age or grade level

Number of Participants

Any number of participants

Equipment

None

Setup

Choose a level playing area, and set boundaries for play depending on the group size.

How to Lead

- Based on surface conditions, decide whether the game will be played at walking, jogging, or running speed.
- Have participants spread out until they are standing at least 5 feet (1.5 m) apart (when they spread out their arms, they should not touch anyone else's arms).
- Explain that the goal is for the tagger (the lead snow crystal) to capture all of the loose snow crystals into one large sinter.
- The lead snow crystal gives chase and tags someone.
- The lead snow crystal and the tagged player hook arms and give chase as a twosome sinter. When they tag a third player, they then give chase as a threesome sinter, and so on.
- The round ends when all snow crystals have been captured into one large sinter.

Variations

- If your group is larger than 20, start with two or three lead snow crystals who create two or three super sinters.
- Super sinter tag can be played on snowshoes as a warm-up or to practice changing direction in an active, engaging way.

Safety Consideration

Based on surface conditions, decide whether the game will be played at walking, jogging, or running speed.

Shoveling Machine

Because we frequently use shovels in the winter environment, this icebreaker is a fun and creative way to get moving. The goal is for small groups to make themselves into a machine that can shovel snow, with as many parts (gears, levers, etc.) as they can devise with their bodies. The machine should have motion and sound and include all group members. The machine often takes the form of an assembly line, but it can be anything participants dream up, such as a snow lifting machine or snow throwing machine.

Age or Grade Level

Any age or grade level

Number of Participants

Any number of participants

Equipment

None

Setup

Choose a level playing area.

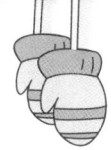

So That's Why It's So Heavy!

A typical shovelful of snow includes over a million snowflakes!

How to Lead

- Divide the large group into even-numbered teams (a size of four to eight participants is ideal).
- Give the teams five minutes to prepare their machines.
- Once the time is up, the teams take turns presenting their machines to the large group.

Variations

- If you have buckets, shovels, sleds, or other such props, the groups could incorporate them into their designs.
- If snow and terrain conditions allow, the shoveling machines could actually move or shovel snow as part of the demonstration.

Snow Shovel Machine Initiative

Snow shovel machine can be progressed into an initiative, or problem-solving, activity in which each small group devises a strategy for moving a load of snow from one location to another.

Age or Grade Level

Grade 5 and up

Number of Participants

Any number of participants

Equipment

- Ski poles, Kool-Aid, or another way of marking snow
- Buckets or containers of various sizes
- Shovels of various sizes
- Sleds or toboggans

Setup

- Choose a level playing area.
- Determine the amount of snow to be moved (a square meter often works well), and mark it out with ski poles or Kool-Aid on the snow.
- Mark the location to where the snow must be moved using ski poles or Kool-Aid.

How to Lead

- Decide whether you want the initiative to be competitive (i.e., the small groups compete to see who can move their snow the fastest or with the fewest trips) or to focus on some other aspect of the activity (e.g., cooperation, teamwork).
- Decide whether to give the small groups planning time.
- Present the guidelines (which will depend on the props you have).
- Give the start signal and watch the snow start to fly.

Yeti Tag

Yetis (also called abominable snowmen) are mythological creatures thought by some to inhabit the Himalaya Mountains, crossing glaciers and high mountain passes. They are often depicted as large white furry creatures that leave big foot-prints in the snow.

Age or Grade Level

Any age or grade level

Number of Participants

Any number of participants

Equipment

Ski poles, cones, or Kool-Aid for marking the boundaries of the playing area

Setup

- Choose a level playing area.
- Mark the boundaries of the playing area.

How to Lead

- Choose two players to be yetis and have them stand between the two boundaries.
- The rest of the players line up along one of the boundaries facing the yetis.

- Play begins when the yetis chant "We're the yetis, if you are ready; if you're wearing . . ." and they choose a color or an item of clothing the players are wearing (e.g., blue, winter hat).

- Any player wearing that item or color must attempt to walk or run across the playing field to get to the opposite boundary without being tagged by a yeti.

- A player who is tagged before reaching the other side becomes a yeti and helps the original yetis tag players in additional rounds.

- Those who make it across without being tagged wait behind that boundary line until the yetis chant again.

- Play continues until everyone is tagged or only two players haven't been tagged.

Safety Considerations

- Based on surface conditions, decide whether the game will be played at walking, jogging, or running speed.

- Allow participants to run in only one direction at a time.

> ### The Search for Yeti
> Alexander the Great, who in 326 BC set out to conquer the Indus Valley, heard stories of the yeti and demanded to see one for himself. But local people told him they were unable to present one because the creatures could not survive at that low an altitude. Indeed, yetis are thought to roam the Himalaya mountain range at an altitude of 14,000 to 20,000 feet.

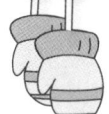

Yeti Frozen Tag

Yeti tag can be progressed into yeti frozen tag.

Age or Grade Level

Any age or grade level

Number of Participants

Any number of participants

Equipment

Ski poles, cones, or Kool-Aid for marking the boundaries of the playing area

Setup

- Choose a level playing area.
- Mark the boundaries of the playing area.

How to Lead

- Choose one or two (or more) players to be yetis, depending on the size of the group.

- Yetis begin the game in the middle of the playing area. Players tagged by yetis must freeze on the spot where they were tagged with their arms and legs open (in a jumping jack position).

- Tagged players remain frozen until another participant ducks or crawls under their arms or legs. Let the game continue for as long as it remains exciting and fun.
- Switch the yetis often.

Safety Consideration

Based on surface conditions, decide whether the game will be played at walking, jogging, or running speed.

Yeti Footprint Track Tag

Sherpas and mountain climbers have long claimed to see yeti footprints in the snow. If you have freshly fallen snow, you have the great fortune of being able to use yeti footprint track tag as an icebreaker. Tell your group that they have all been temporarily transformed into yetis who must navigate a mountain pass together.

Age or Grade Level

Any age or grade level

Number of Participants

Any number of participants

Equipment

Kool-Aid, cones, or poly spots to mark base camps and yeti caves

Setup

Choose a level playing area.

How to Lead

- Have the players (yetis) line up, one behind the other, with their hands on the shoulders of the yeti in front of them.
- Have the group stomp out a series of paths or tracks in the snow that intersect at regular intervals.
- Keep the path fairly narrow, but have them stomp out a few wider yeti cave and base camp areas in which to pass, rest, or be safe.
- Once you have a track that is big enough and complex enough to fit the size of your group, choose one or two (or more) players to remain yetis while the rest of the players become sherpas and climbers.
- Identify the areas on the track that are base camps (safe zones) and yeti caves (where passing is allowed) using Kool-Aid, cones, or poly spots.
- Explain that all players must remain in the yeti footprint tracks and that passing may occur only in the yeti cave areas.
- Climbers may remain in base camp for a maximum of 10 seconds before they have to move back out onto the tracks. When a yeti tags a sherpa or climber, they

exchange roles. Immediate tag-backs are not allowed. Let the game continue for as long as it remains exciting and fun. Switch the yetis often if they are having trouble tagging sherpas or climbers.

- Play continues until everyone is tagged or only two players haven't been tagged.

Variation

Yeti footprint track tag can be played on snowshoes as a warm-up or to practice changing direction in an active, engaging way.

Safety Consideration

Based on surface conditions, decide whether the game will be played at walking, jogging, or running speed.

Sherpa Winter Walk

Sherpas often guide climbers through rugged terrain in the mountains of Nepal. This icebreaker is a blindfolded winter adventure in which "sherpas" guide the group through and around obstacles found or made in the environment.

Age or Grade Level

Any age or grade level

Number of Participants

Any number of participants

Equipment

None

Setup

Choose a location that has access to several kinds of obstacles such as snow banks, trees, or park benches.

How to Lead

- Break the participants into groups of 8 to 10, each of which has a sherpa. (If there are 10 or fewer participants, you will be the sherpa.)
- Line up the players in each group, one behind the other, with their hands on the shoulders of the person in front of them.
- If players are comfortable, they can close their eyes, wear a blindfold, or drop their hats down over their eyes.
- The sherpa is sighted and guides the group through, around, and over obstacles such as snow banks, snow trenches, and trees. The group follows the sherpa in a line.
- Sherpas can describe the obstacles as part of a winter adventure story such as crevasses, icefalls, glaciers, and the like.

- The group follows along and listens to the sherpa's descriptions for clues about what to expect and what to do (e.g., crawl over something, duck under a branch, roll in the snow).
- The players soon learn that they need to depend on, support, and communicate with each other to negotiate the obstacles.

Safety Considerations

- This activity requires participants to trust each other and work as a team to ensure everyone's safety while traversing the course. Make sure that your group is ready for this responsibility.
- If an obstacle requires players to be off the ground, have adequate sighted spotters at the obstacle to assist.

Polar Bears and Sled Dogs

In the Arctic, many expeditions use sled dogs to traverse the snow and ice. Some sled dogs are known for their talent in spotting polar bears and alerting expedition members. Occasionally, polar bears and sled dogs have been seen playing together, chasing each other to and fro. This active icebreaker involves the polar bears chasing the sled dogs, and vice versa, whenever their team name is mentioned in a story.

Age or Grade Level

Any age or grade level

Number of Participants

Any number of participants

Equipment

Ski poles, cones, or Kool-Aid for marking the boundaries of the playing area

Setup

- Choose a level playing area.
- Mark the boundaries of the playing area.

How to Lead

- Split the group into two teams: polar bears and sled dogs.
- In the middle of the playing area, have the polar bears line up parallel to the sled dogs (facing each other), with about 3 feet (1 m) between them.
- Tell a story about polar exploration. Whenever you say *polar bear* in the story, the polar bears have to run back to their boundary line.
- The sled dogs try to tag the polar bears before they reach the boundary line.
- A polar bear tagged by the sled dogs becomes a sled dog and joins that team.

- When you say *sled dog* in your story, the polar bears try to tag the sled dogs before they reach their boundary line.
- Play for a set amount of time or until one team has tagged everyone of the opposing team.

Variation

Polar bears and sled dogs can be played on snowshoes as a warm-up or to practice changing direction in an active, engaging way.

Safety Consideration

Based on surface conditions, decide whether the game will be played at walking, jogging, or running speed.

Snowshoe Hare, Snowshoe Hare, Arctic Fox

Snowshoe hare, snowshoe hare, arctic fox is a winter adaptation of the much-loved duck, duck, goose. Both the snowshoe hare and the arctic fox are hardy animals that thrive in the winter environment. Their coats change color to snow-white every winter to help them camouflage, and both have feet that are specially adapted to snow travel. This active icebreaker allows the group to have fun, warm up, and learn about two active winter mammals.

Age or Grade Level

Any age or grade level

Number of Participants

Any number of participants

Equipment

None

Setup

- Choose a level playing area
- Break larger groups into smaller circles of 12 to 15 players.

Snowshoe Hares

Snowshoe hares have large, furry feet that help them to traverse winter landscapes. Over a period of about ten weeks, the snowshoe hare's white winter coat turns brown when the snow melts in the spring. They feed at night and are very fast—all the better to escape the foxes and other creatures that prey on them!

How to Lead

- Have each group form a circle, facing inward. The players can stand or sit if you have brought sit-upons.
- Select a volunteer to be "it" for each circle.
- The person who is "it" starts the game by walking around outside the circle and tapping each player's head (if players are sitting) or shoulder (if players are standing). The person names each player "snowshoe hare," "snowshoe hare," "snowshoe hare," until naming one "arctic fox."

- The arctic fox chases the person who is "it" around the outside of the circle in an attempt to tag. If tagged, the person who is "it" continues in the role. If the "it" person makes it to arctic fox's spot before getting tagged, the arctic fox is now "it" and starts a new game by walking on the outside of the circle.

Variation

Snowshoe hare, snowshoe hare, arctic fox can be played on snowshoes as a warm-up or to practice changing direction in an active, engaging way.

Safety Consideration

Based on surface conditions, decide whether the game will be played at walking, jogging, or running speed.

Snowshoe Hare, Arctic Fox, Polar Bear

Snowshoe hare, arctic fox, polar bear is a winter adaptation of rock-paper-scissors. The snowshoe hare, arctic fox, and polar bear are all no strangers to the cold, white winter world. They are all an integral part of the Arctic ecosystem. This icebreaker involves two teams who act as one of the three mammals in a fun, team-based version of tag.

Age or Grade Level

Any age or grade level

Number of Participants

Any number of participants

Equipment

Ski poles, cones, or Kool-Aid for marking the boundaries of the playing area

Setup

- Choose a level playing area.
- Mark the center line and end lines of the playing area.

How to Lead

- Introduce the group to the three mammals, and have them practice the motions and sounds each mammal will make during the game.
  - Snowshoe hare: Crouch down very low to the ground, put your thumbs in your ears, and make a thumping sound: *Thump, thump!*
  - Arctic fox: Crouch slightly, make a pouncing wavelike motion with your arms in front of your chest, and bark: *Wooowooo!*
  - Polar bear: Stand on tippy toes with your arms above your head and make a menacing growling noise: *Rawrrrr!*
- Break the group into two teams.

- Have each team huddle up and decide which mammal to act out together.
- When both teams are ready, have them line up facing each other, about 5 feet (1.5 m) from the center line.
- Call out, "One, two, three, Go Winter!"
- Each team then in unison acts out the mammal they chose (snowshoe hare, arctic fox, or polar bear). The following determines the winning team:
  - Snowshoe hares beat arctic foxes.
  - Arctic foxes beat polar bears.
  - Polar bears beat snowshoe hares.
- The winners try to tag the losers and bring them over to their side. The losers are safe if they make it back to their boundary line without being taged.
- If both teams show the same mammal, no one wins and the teams return to their huddle to choose a mammal for the next round.
- Rounds continue until one team is completely captured by the other.

Variation

Snowshoe hare, arctic fox, polar bear can be played on snowshoes as a warm-up or to practice changing direction in an active, engaging way.

Safety Consideration

Based on surface conditions, decide whether the game will be played at walking, jogging, or running speed.

Chickadee Perch

The black-capped chickadee is a cute and hardy bird, often seen at both backyard feeders and in forested areas in winter. These small birds can be recognized by their black caps and throats and by their call. The black-capped chickadee was named for its call, which can be heard in winter, a rapid *chickadee-dee-dee-dee*. It is also known for its acrobatic antics. This icebreaker turns the group into chickadees on perches for a rousing winter adaptation of musical chairs.

Age or Grade Level

Any age or grade level

Number of Participants

Any number of participants

Equipment

None

Setup

- Choose a level playing area.
- Break larger groups into smaller circles of 20 to 30 participants.

Chickadee Calls

The more "dee" notes at the end of a chickadee call, the more agitated the bird is becoming. For instance, a chickadee may end their call with just one "dee" when a known person fills a favorite bird feeder, but an owl roosting near the feeding station would warrant many more "dee" notes.

How to Lead

- Have each group form a circle, facing inward.
- Ask everyone to get a partner.
- Each pair decides who is the chickadee and who is the perch.
- Have all the chickadees stand in a circle and all the perches stand in a circle surrounding the chickadees.
- Have the chickadees practice their call: *chickadee-dee-dee-dee*.
- Have all the perches practice their perch stances (usually on one knee, making a perch out of the other leg, but other creative stances may work).
- At your signal, the chickadees walk clockwise around the circle and the perches walk counterclockwise. While walking, the chickadees flap their wings and make their *chickadee-dee-dee-dee* call.
- When you say "Find your perch," each chickadee must find a perch and sit on it.
- The last pair to pair up must change roles, with the chickadee becoming the perch and vice versa.
- Play several rounds until most pairs have changed roles.

Variation

Chickadee perch can be played on snowshoes as a warm-up or to practice changing direction in an active, engaging way.

Safety Consideration

Based on surface conditions, decide whether the game will be played at walking, jogging, or running speed.

Chapter 5

Place-Based and First Nations Activities

The activities in this chapter are intended not only to get people outside but also (and more important) to ensure that their experience outdoors is enjoyable and memorable. The place-based activities in this chapter are for use outside a community or recreation center, in a schoolyard, on a local playing field, or at a base camp. They help people become accustomed to and familiar with being outside in winter conditions; think of it as acclimatizing! Participants learn what they need to do to be comfortable while being active outside in winter.

We would be remiss if we didn't acknowledge the First Nations groups throughout the world. The term *First Nations* refers to indigenous people living in geographic areas preceding colonization. These people survived by being intimately connected with the land and sea, the rhythms of nature. Their attunement with these rhythms comes not only from their knowledge of but also from their respect for the natural world. What can we gain today by considering First Nations past practices?

This chapter includes a series of challenging First Nations activities that reveal the strength, muscular endurance, and overall fitness required to survive in a hostile environment. In environments with extended cold seasons, people were traditionally confined to small areas such as igloos and snow houses, so most of the activities in this chapter are performed in small areas. These traditional activities reflect the importance of both play and fitness in indigenous culture.

Place-Based Activities

Winter Walks and Wildlife Camouflage

A basic premise of being comfortable outdoors in winter is moving enough to be warm but not so much that you sweat, which is extremely dangerous. Walking is an ideal activity for reaching this balance.

That's a Lot of Snowmen!

In 2015 Ottawa broke the world record for amount of snowmen built in one hour, totaling 1,299. But the people of Iiyama, Japan, beat their record only two weeks later when more than 600 people gathered to make 1,585 snowmen.

Age or Grade Level

Any age or grade level

Number of Participants

Any number of participants

Equipment

Wildlife cutouts and lists of cutouts

Setup

- Make sure you are familiar with the route, hazards, and route alternatives.
- Ensure that participants are dressed to suit the current and potential conditions.

How to Lead

- Identify a lead (leader) and sweep (last person in line) for the walk.
- All participants should stay behind the lead and ahead of the sweep.
- Plan a route that includes points of interest, challenges, and activities to add purpose and interest to the walk.

Variations

- This basic activity may be supplemented with other activities in this book (e.g., snowshoe walk, Nordic ski touring, winter trekking).
- Intrigue can be added to any outdoor trek by adding wildlife sightings. Consider placing life-size cutouts of birds and other animals within 5 to 15 feet (1.5 to 4.6 m) of the trail. Give participants a list of potential sightings before beginning the excursion. At the midpoint of the journey, the group may review sightings; on the return route, each cutout can be revealed and collected.

Safety Considerations

- Throughout the walk, monitor body temperatures through observation and by inquiring periodically.
- In areas without wind and in difficult sections, slow the pace to avoid sweating; in exposed areas, increase the pace to avoid chilling.
- Slips and falls are a winter concern. Avoid extremely slippery areas, or have everyone in the group wear crampons.
- Carry a leader pack (see chapter 3 for what to include).

Whiteout/Camouflage

This is a popular activity that can be done to slow the pace or bring the group together along the trail. Simply put, it is a hide and seek activity in which the catcher stays in one spot while the players try to hide, or camouflage themselves, so the catcher cannot see them. Leaders or participants may choose the name ("whiteout," "blizzard," or "camouflage") that they feel suits their group and location best.

Age or Grade Level

Any age or grade level

Number of Participants

Any number of participants

Equipment

None

Setup

- Choose an area with obstacles suitable for hiding, and identify clear boundaries for play.
- Have participants walk through the play area to familiarize themselves and also to create lots of tracks on the snow so that the catcher cannot use the first tracks of the game to locate players.

How to Lead

- The catcher calls "Lights out" and closes his or her eyes for 20 to 30 seconds, counting aloud.
- During this time players move away from the catcher and find hiding places that permit them to see the catcher (i.e., they are camouflaged).
- At the end of the lights-out count, the catcher calls out "Spotting" or "Searching" to indicate that he or she is now looking for players.
- The catcher must remain in place but may rotate to try to spot players.
- Players may attempt to walk toward the catcher when the catcher is not looking in their direction and then freeze to camouflage themselves when the catcher looks in their direction. They may also choose to stay in their original hiding places.
- When all possible hiders have been spotted, the catcher holds one, two, three, four, or five fingers overhead and rotates, calling out "Code out" to indicate that the code is visible. Hiders take note of the code, and the catcher has a final opportunity to identify more hiders.
- After showing the code, the catcher calls "All in," and all hiders approach the catcher one by one and whisper the code. Anyone who whispers the wrong code is caught.
- The group may decide the formula for who becomes the next catcher.

Variation

This is an ideal activity for creating a change of pace or slowing down a group when out for a walk, ski, or snowshoe. The activity may be played at different times in different places along the travel route.

Safety Consideration

Avoid cutover areas—previously forested areas that are now open or lacking trees. Sizes of cutovers vary. The danger of cutovers in winter is that snow-covered tree stumps may be invisible on the surface, and serious injury can result when people plunge suddenly into the snow.

Bird Feeding

Establishing a series of bird-feeding stations gives reason and purpose to going outside, even in harsh conditions. When participants have a goal (such as feeding birds), weather is often a superfluous by-product, just another challenge or even something that enhances the experience.

What Do Birds Eat?

In most areas, black-oil sunflower seeds are the most popular for attracting a wide variety of species. Finches, chickadees, titmice, cardinals, nuthatches, and many other common feeder birds will gobble it up! Millet is attractive to ground-feeding birds like doves and juncos. Suet can attract magnificent woodpeckers!

Age or Grade Level

Any age or grade level

Number of Participants

Any number of participants

Equipment

Birdfeed and bird feeders

Setup

Establish bird-feeding stations and feeding routines before winter begins.

How to Lead

- The whole group can go to each station along a regular route.
- This is a long-term activity that should engage participants for at least the fall and winter seasons. Participants must be aware that failure to fulfill their responsibilities can be catastrophic to birds, who come to depend on the food they provide.
- Discuss means of attracting birds to new feeders; then implement participants' suggestions and consider the results.

Variations

- Have participants make their own feeding stations and feeding arrangements (see www.kidactivities.net/category/theme-birds.aspx for suggestions).
- Rather than have the whole group tend to the stations, divide the group into smaller groups and give each a responsibility such as preparing the birdfeed, tending the feeders, recording feeder activity, tracking birds, or noting signs of predator activity.

Safety Consideration

Check the long-range forecast before restocking bird-feeding stations. In the event of impending poor weather, leave adequate feed to sustain the birds during snow days, to avoid having to make excursions in marginal conditions.

Snow Carnival: Snow Art

In this activity participants create out of snow anything from a convertible car to a work of art. Other suggestions are machines, trucks, trains, a theme park, animal sculptures, creative sculptures, a wax/snow museum of famous people, an art show, a cityscape, a landscape, a logo, a pyramid, a trophy case, and Christmas-themed creations.

Age or Grade Level

Any age or grade level

Number of Participants

Any number of participants

Equipment

- Shovels, buckets, and sleds can be used, but not all are essential.
- Three spray bottles (one for each primary color) filled with colored water; use food coloring, Kool-Aid, or Jell-O for color agents
- Old handsaws or rectangular buckets or containers if creating snow blocks

Setup

Because this is a larger, longer-term project, check your local forecast to ensure that the weather remains suitable for constructing the snow art.

How to Lead

- This activity may require more than one session; hence, participants should develop detailed construction plans.
- Divide large groups into smaller groups and assign tasks to individuals and small groups. Whenever possible, give participants free rein to run the show and let their creativity shine through.
- If necessary, assign tasks to specific individuals or groups to encourage them to take full ownership and pride in the construction.
- Encourage those who finish early to help others.

Variations

- Link this to school or community winter days, a winter carnival, or seasonal celebrations.
- Snow art may include snow painting using spray bottles containing food coloring or Jell-O powder.

Safety Consideration

Be careful on walking surfaces after glazing (spraying snow with water or colored water).

Snow Globe

Snow Globe is a multicurriculur activity in which participants make their own globe of the world out of snow. Once the sphere is created, relief features such as mountain ranges may be carved and countries, land masses, and bodies of water may be colored. Students are encouraged to be creative in their approach and work.

Who's Afraid to Go Out in the Snow?

Did you know there is an official snow phobia? Chionophobia, from the Greek *chion* (snow) and *phobos* (fear), is the persistent fear of being trapped in the snow.

Age or Grade Level

Any age or grade level

Number of Participants

Any number of participants

Equipment

Spray bottles filled with colored water (use food coloring, Kool-Aid, or Jell-O for color agents)

Setup

For this activity, you will need snow that is wet enough to bond (i.e., make a snowball) and a large open area with a gradual slope.

How to Lead

- At the top of the slope, make a snowball 2 to 3 feet (0.6 to 1 m) in diameter.
- Roll the snowball down the slope until it is 4 to 7 feet (1.2 to 2 m) in diameter.
- Set snow at the base of the snowball (i.e., the globe) to keep it from moving.
- Carve rough edges off to make the globe round.
- Mark continents on the globe; then color them with colored water.

Variation

Rather than making a globe, cut the front of the ball to make a flat surface and use colored water to draw your community, school, or group emblem.

Safety Consideration

No participants should be in front of the ball when it is being pushed down the slope.

Snobsticle (Snow Obstacle) Course

Snobsticle is an activity in which leaders and participants may be creative in establishing their own obstacle course using local features and terrain. The leaders must ensure the course is safe while the participants invent and create.

Age or Grade Level

Any age or grade level

Number of Participants

Any number of participants

Equipment

Shovels, buckets, sleds

Setup

With the help of the group, choose a start line and finish line for your obstacle course.

How to Lead

- Divide the group into smaller groups, each of which is responsible for designing and building one obstacle for the course.
- Sample obstacles include a tunnel, free run in deep snow, snowshoe track, scooter, sled haul, snow wall, Everest climb, glissade (descending moderate snow slopes under control by sliding on one's feet or rump), and maze.
- Choose obstacles and obstacle sequences that suit the age and abilities of participants.

Variations

- Once participants have gone through this process once, let them design and sequence their own obstacle course.
- For very large groups, consider dividing the group in half and having each group build an obstacle course; the groups then challenge each other to navigate the courses.

Safety Considerations

- Make sure the area is free of ice and other potential hazards. You should approve all obstacles at each stage (choice, design, building).
- Use caution if there is a risk of participants falling in areas in which there is a thick or hard crust on snow.

Snow Maze

The snow maze is an ideal activity for a large multiage group. This activity works best when one group designs and builds while another group is the user group that will navigate the maze. Older participants construct the maze for younger participants to enjoy.

Age or Grade Level

Any age or grade level

Number of Participants

Any number of participants

Equipment

Shovels, buckets, sleds

Setup

If possible, design your maze on paper before beginning.

How to Lead

- Assign individuals or groups to each area of maze design and construction.
- Build the maze with snow trenches that are 2 or 3 feet (0.6 to 1 m) deep so that participants go through on their abdomens or on hands and knees. The idea is to keep them low enough that they cannot look over the top.
- Begin with the start and exit of the maze, and follow this with a series of passages, junctions, and bottlenecks. Try to fill all available space.
- Divide your maze into sections with only one bottleneck that serves as the exit from one area and the entrance to the next area.

Variations

Square, spiral, or vortex mazes

Safety Consideration

Participants who are not comfortable in small or confined spaces may be given an alternate route. Another option is to permit them to go through with a partner with the choice to exit standing if necessary.

Snow Shelter: Quinzhee

Snow shelters can be made with any age group. The older the participants are, the smaller the group you will need. Most important is completing the quinzhee so participants have a sense of accomplishment and a thorough understanding of the process.

Age or Grade Level

Any age or grade level

Number of Participants

Any number of participants

Equipment

Shovels, buckets, sleds

Setup

Select a flat, protected area with plenty of snow nearby.

How to Lead

- Have participants shovel snow into a mound 6 to 7 feet (1.8 to 2.1 m) high with an 8- to 10-foot (2.4 to 3 m) diameter base (this is a suitable size for a midsize group of 5 to 10 builders).
- Once the mound is complete, builders pack the snow down with shovels or hands.
- Next, builders push spaghetti noodles (or twigs) perpendicularly into the exterior wall of the entire shelter, approximately 12 inches (30 cm) apart. The length of the noodle represents the thickness of the shelter wall.
- If this is just a learning activity, proceed directly to the next stage. If the shelter is to be used, the mound should be left for two to three hours to allow the snow crystals to bond (sinter), which decreases the risk of its caving in.
- Builders dig out a shelter entrance.
- Builders then dig in and up, all the way to the noodles or twigs.
- When working with younger or newer groups, you may have to dig in when things slow down. This may mean doing much of the digging. As participants become more engaged, you can then guide them in the work. It is most important that participants experience the result of their efforts.

Variation

Once the quinzhee is completed, consider other uses for the shelter (e.g., a staging area for the Inuit games presented later in this chapter).

Safety Consideration

Make sure builders dig up as they dig in to avoid excessive snow load overhead. Avoid being in the shelter with a large mound of snow load overhead.

Native (Inuit) and Northern Games

Native games have been passed down from generation to generation for millennia. The limitations of Arctic weather and the Inuits' small living space encouraged the development of many games. Most traditional Inuit games involve competition between two people in an atmosphere of friendship and fun. These games require strength, concentration, coordination, agility, and flexibility—all qualities that are essential for a traditional hunting and survival lifestyle.

Although the movements required for most native games may seem simple, some can be quite difficult to master. Mastering these activities requires talent, practice, and most of all, encouragement. Participants are driven to improve by continually putting their best foot forward. Make sure all participants have some success in their preliminary attempts at these activities, and emphasize the importance of positive, constructive feedback (from all participants). Even in competitions, encouraging athletes not only pushes them to do their best but also models good sporting behavior. The greatest reward is not always winning.

Originally played in unstructured settings with basic rules that varied from region to region, today many native games have accepted general rules and are played in more structured events such as the Labrador Winter Games, Arctic Games, and North Coast Sports meets. Competitions like these have always been a significant part of community life that gives participants a chance to showcase their talents while reflecting the special abilities of their people. This display of cultural talent is a humbling experience to elders and inspirational to youth. The tea doll is the traditional award given to the team that earns the most points in the Native Games Competition at the Fall/Winter Sportsmeet.

Following are important etiquette rules for developing social skills during native games:

- Treat your fellow participants with respect.
- Always encourage others to do their best.
- Compliment others on their efforts.
- Give maximum effort and maximum participation.

We encourage you to find traditional indigenous activities in your local area. In some cases, activities from different parts of the globe are similar, but names differ and variations exist.

During your presentation, teachable moments, and debriefing, consider eliciting insights from your participants, such as cultural relevance, the significance of activities and play in cold climates and in confined spaces, and the connections with practical activities such as hunting. For example, owl hop, the first activity in this unit, develops leg strength and power, which are important for quick accelerations in a chase. The second activity, seal crawl, develops stealth and the skills of slithering and crawling on snow or ice. These skills contribute to hunting success. Consider asking questions such as the following:

- What muscle groups or fitness components are developed in this activity?
- What indigenous activity (e.g., hunting seals) could this activity relate to?
- Why do you think indigenous people played this game?

Owl Hop

The owl hop is a test of strength and muscular endurance.

Age or Grade Level

Any age or grade level

Number of Participants

Any number of participants

Equipment

None

Setup

Select a relatively level area with snow that is consistent in both depth and hardness/softness.

How to Lead

- The object of this activity is to outlast opponents in continuously hopping on one foot.
- Only one leg is used throughout the activity.
- Participants stand on one foot with the instep of the opposite foot behind the standing knee; the nonhopping foot must remain in place.
- On your cue, participants hop (foot must come off the snow) continuously on one foot.
- The winner is the person who outlasts all the others.

Variations

- Use upbeat music and a judge.
- Allow participants to gently bump each other.

Safety Consideration

Start the lesson with a warm-up activity (such as a large group game), and have participants stretch all major muscle groups before and after the activity (with emphasis on calves, hamstrings, buttocks, quads, shoulders, and fingers).

Seal Crawl

The seal crawl was traditionally done outdoors on hard snow or ice; it simulates stealth in approaching wildlife.

Age or Grade Level

Any age or grade level

Number of Participants

Any number of participants

Equipment

None

Setup

Designate a snow-covered area suitable to the age and strength of the participants. For teenage boys and girls, a distance between the start and finish lines of approximately 20 and 12 meters, respectively, is suitable.

How to Lead

- The object of this activity is to be the first to cross the finish line.
- To begin, participants lie belly down with their noses on the start line, their hands under their shoulders, and their feet crossed.

- On your start command, participants straighten their arms and move their outstretched, stiff bodies (no knee bending) forward by using just their hands.
- The winner is the first person (nose) to cross the finish line using proper form.

Variations

- Shorten the distance for beginners so they can make it all the way to the finish line. As participants become better at the movement, you can increase the distance gradually until they can go all the way. However, you want participants to be successful in the beginning to maintain their interest so they can increase their ability.
- Separating boys and girls gives both a chance to compete against those of equal stature. It also allows you to adjust the distance of the race accordingly.

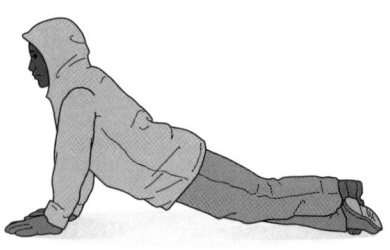

- With bigger classes, divide the boys and girls into groups of 6 to 10 and have the top two or three finishers in each heat race against each other in a final round. Alternate boy and girl races to give participants a break.
- Present this activity as a challenge event rather than a competitive event.

Safety Consideration

Participants may use knee pads if the surface is too hard.

Leg Wrestling

Leg wrestling is a test of strength and strategy. In some native cultures, leg wrestling signified the transition to manhood.

Age or Grade Level

Any age or grade level

Number of Participants

Any number of participants; the activity is done in pairs.

Equipment

None

Setup

This activity is best played in an area with a bedding of soft snow.

How to Lead

- Opponents lie side by side, in opposite directions, and interlock their inside arms.
- On a count of 3, opponents bring up their inside legs and interlock them at the knee region.

- The object of this activity is to cause the opponent to roll over while you remain flat on the snow. The best strategy is to quickly hook the opponent by the knee to gain the advantage.
- The winner is the person who wins two of three contests.
- The first contest is done with the right leg; the second, with the left. If a third is necessary, a coin toss determines which leg is used; the first winner calls the side of the coin.
- After all participants have had a chance to compete, gather them together to discuss issues that arose in the competitions and strategies that worked (e.g., leg length, quickness of the upward leg movement, power, hamstring flexibility, hooking the opponent's leg).

Variations

Leg wrestling may be done as a competitive tournament, knockout, double elimination, ongoing ladder tournament, or participatory experiential activity.

Safety Consideration

Provide a proper warm-up to minimize the risk of injury.

Finger Hang

The object of this activity is to hang from a horizontal pole by one finger for the longest time.

Age or Grade Level

Any age or grade level

Number of Participants

Any number of participants; the activity is done in groups of three or more.

Equipment

One pole (e.g., broom handle) per group (at least 2 feet, or 1.5 m, long)

Setup

Two people hold either end of a pole about 4 feet (1.2 m) high.

How to Lead

- The competitor grabs the pole with the middle finger and, with the other hand, grabs the wrist of the hand hanging from the pole.
- Legs are lifted off the snow and crossed or in a kneeling position.
- Feet must be off the snow as the two carriers move slowly forward and timing starts.
- The participants holding the pole may also kneel on the snow to keep the person off the snow.

Variations

- This is very difficult to perform with just one finger. Another option is to hold on to the pole with one or two hands.
- Place the pole on a fixed platform (so it does not move), and have participants see how long they can hold on (using one or two hands).
- Rather than the pole remaining in one position, the two people holding the pole travel forward; with this variation the winning team is the group that moves the greatest distance while the person hanging on to the pole is off the snow.

Safety Considerations

- The two people holding the pole must have a solid grip so as not to drop the person hanging on.
- A series of commands and responses is recommended for activities that involve multiple participants in different roles. Here are examples for the finger hang:
  - *Handle secure* (said by the people holding the pole)
  - *Ready to hang on* (said by the person performing the finger hang)
  - *Hang on* (said by the people holding the pole)
  - *Hanging on* (said by the person performing the finger hang)

Labrador Hurdles

The object of this activity is to jump as many hurdles as possible using two-foot hops over a series of hurdles laid out in a straight line. Once they have completed the series of hurdles, competitors turn and repeat the line of hurdles without breaking the rhythm. Competitors must clear the hurdle with a two-foot hop and land on the other side with both feet touching the snow at the same time. They must continue with the same rhythm until they knock a hurdle down, break rhythm, or become exhausted and cannot continue. There is no time restriction for this event.

Age or Grade Level

Any age or grade level

Number of Participants

Any number of participants

Equipment

None

Setup

Participants make the hurdles from snow; they should be approximately 2 feet (60 cm) wide, 6 inches (15 cm) thick, and 18 inches (45 cm) high (you can adjust the height based on the age or size of your participants). Six to ten hurdles in a straight line are suitable, with approximately 15 inches (38 cm) to 2 feet (60 cm) between hurdles depending on the age or size of your participants. Testing participants' vertical and horizontal hopping distance can help determine the best dimensions for the course.

How to Lead

- To begin, have participants experiment by hopping over a single hurdle to coordinate their arm swings with the two-foot hopping motion.
- Next, have them hop over a series of hurdles without changing direction.
- Now have the participant hop over two hurdles, change direction, and hop back.
- This is a good time to discuss strategies for hopping longer (e.g., using the arms for momentum, swinging the legs to the side or over the top).
- Review the rules and give examples of what judges should look for (break of rhythm, the turn of direction). In pairs (one performing and one judging and recording), participants take turns hopping over hurdles.
- Set up a chart, or have the participants chart their own improvements over the season.

Safety Consideration

Ensure that the hopping surface is not slippery.

Side Reach

The object of this activity is to place a small block of wood as far to the side as possible and retrieve it.

Age or Grade Level

Any age or grade level

Number of Participants

Any number of participants

Equipment

Small block of wood and measuring tape

Setup

Mark out a 15-inch (38 cm) right angle in the snow to guide participants' foot positions for the activity. Heels should be at one line, and the side of one foot should be beside the line that is perpendicular to the heel line. If the left arm is used to reach, the left foot is placed adjacent to the side marker.

How to Lead

- Participants who are right-handed hold a block of wood in the right hand and put the left hand behind the back (vice versa for those who are left-handed, or participants may choose the side they prefer).
- The right hand holding the block of wood goes behind the knees as the competitor places the wood as far on the left side as possible (and parallel to the toes).

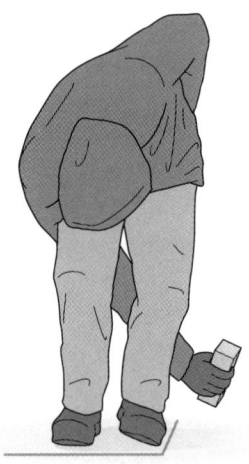

- Another participant records the distance of the placement, and the competitor then retrieves the block of wood in the same manner.
- Three attempts are permitted. If the block of wood is dropped, it counts as a try.
- Participants may not touch the snow with the hand during any part of the maneuver.
- To begin, have participants experiment by performing the reach with both the right hand and the left hand without the block of wood. This will help them determine which side they are most comfortable with. You can also have all participants perform first from the right and then from the left.
- Give participants 10 minutes to experiment and strategize with a partner.
- In pairs, the participants now test their skill (one performing while the other judges).
- This should be performed on a line on the snow.
- The judge measures the distance with a measuring tape and ensures that the competitor performs the skill correctly.

Safety Consideration

An appropriate stretching warm-up is recommended.

Airplane

The object of this activity is to go the farthest in the shortest amount of time.

Age or Grade Level

Any age or grade level

Number of Participants

Any number of participants; the activity is done in groups of four.

Equipment

Timing and measuring devices

Setup

- The competitor lies facedown with arms straight out to the sides and feet firmly together, keeping the body firm and rigid.
- Three people lift the competitor: one holding both feet, and the other two on each arm.
- The competitor must remain rigid until the body is raised 2 to 3 feet (0.6 to 1 m) above snow.
- When the body sags, the abdomen should just touch the snow (this is a good indicator of the height the competitor should be lifted).

How to Lead

- To begin, participants practice supporting the weight by doing the following:
  - Lifting just the shoulders and remaining stationary
  - Doing a full lift and remaining stationary
  - Doing a full lift and traveling a short distance
- The competitor is carried in this position as far as possible.
- The competitor's body must not sag. The shoulders must not drop below the arms, and the elbows must not bend.
- Distance is measured, but the event is also timed because some carriers walk faster than others.
- Carriers should try to keep a steady pace.

Variation

To make the carry less strenuous for the competitor, have the carriers hold the arms at the elbows.

Safety Considerations

- The lifters must move slowly and steadily and lift with their legs.
- An appropriate stretching warm-up is recommended.

Stick Jump

The object of this activity is to hold a stick with arms about shoulder-width apart and using an overhand grip and jump over it as many times as possible. From a squatted or standing position, participants jump over the stick without letting go of it, and then back again. Repetitions should be continuous without any pause for rest. One backward and forward jump is a considered a successful jump.

Age or Grade Level

Any age or grade level

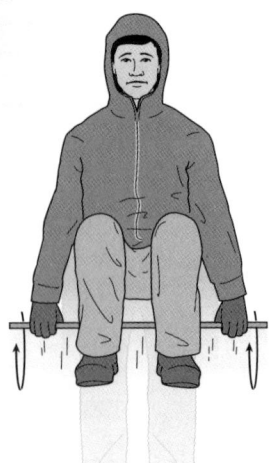

Number of Participants

Any number of participants

Equipment

Broom handle or similar stick that is at least 2 feet (0.6 m) long

Setup

Ensure that snow is packed in the jumping area.

How to Lead

- Participants should start with light jumping.
- They can then progress to jumping up and driving the knees into the chest.
- The next task is jumping with the stick in one hand.
- Finally, participants jump with the stick in both hands.
- The winner is the person who performs the most jumps.

Variation

Beginners may use pieces of a broken hula hoop. The curve makes jumping easier so that they can concentrate on timing the jump and swinging the arms together.

Safety Consideration

Ensure that the area surrounding the jumper is free of obstacles.

Foot Pull

The object of this activity is to pull a competitor over the line or cause the strap or belt to come off. This is a very low-organized game in that participants can perform without any lead-up.

Age or Grade Level

Any age or grade level

Number of Participants

Any number of participants; the activity is performed in pairs.

Equipment

One strap or belt for each pair

Setup

- Mark a line in the snow to separate pairs of competitors and identify each participant's territory.
- Opponents sit on the snow on either side of the line with one leg straight out and the other bent at the knee.
- The strap or belt (securely tape any buckles) is attached to the upturned foot of each opponent, about 2 or 3 feet (0.6 to 1 m) apart.

How to Lead

- On your signal, the opponents pull against each other using their full body strength including arms.
- The player who pulls an opponent over the line or causes the strap or belt to come off wins the contest.
- The winner is the person who wins two of three contests.
- Once everyone has had the opportunity to try the pull, you can discuss strategies for using the arms and untethered leg to obtain maximal pulling power.

Variation

A loop made of webbing may be used in lieu of a belt or strap.

Safety Consideration

Wider webbing (1 or 2 in., or 2.5 to 5 cm) is recommended to avoid compromising the circulation in the foot.

Musk Ox Fight

Two participants begin on all fours in the middle of a circle with heads placed under each other's collarbones so that shoulders are pressed together and heads are tucked under. Using body weight and strength, opponents try to push each other out of the circle. This is a very low-organized game that participants can perform without any lead-up.

Age or Grade Level

Any age or grade level

Number of Participants

Any number of participants; the activity is performed in pairs.

Equipment

None

Setup

Mark a circle (approximately 12 ft, or 3.7 m, in diameter) in the snow.

How to Lead

- The winner is the person who wins two of three contests
- Once everyone has had the opportunity to try the fight, you can discuss strategies for using the arms and legs to obtain maximal pushing power.

Variation

If performed indoors, participants should remove their shoes and wrestle in their socks.

Safety Consideration

Hats (without brims) can be worn to soften the contact between participants' heads.

Monkey Dance

The object of this activity is to outlast the other competitors by doing the monkey dance for the longest period of time.

Age or Grade Level

Any age or grade level

Number of Participants

Any number of participants

Equipment

None

Setup

Participants assume a squatting position with one leg extended in front of them and the heel touching the snow.

How to Lead

- Have participants start the activity with both hands on the snow to support their weight. They can then extend their arms outward for balance.
- On your cue, participants must switch leg positions in a repetitive motion by bringing the extended leg underneath and extending the other.
- Switching leg positions should be in a continuous motion.
- The winner is the person who performs the motion for the longest period of time.

Variations

- Because this task can be difficult, you may need to modify it for some participants. One option is to have them hold on to a skipping rope held by a partner.
- Depending on participants' ability, you may want to have them perform two contests—one with the arms up and one with the arms supporting their weight.

Safety Consideration

Participants with knee issues should be cautious or avoid this activity depending on the type and severity of the issue.

Inuit Push-Up

The object of this activity is to press the person as many times as possible.

Age or Grade Level

Any age or grade level

Number of Participants

Any number of participants; the activity is performed in groups of three or four.

Equipment

None

Setup

- One person lies faceup on the snow with feet outstretched and arms beside the head, palms up.
- A second person stands on the first person's hands, facing that person's feet. A third person stands over the first person (facing the head) to act as a brace and support for the second person, who is lifted.

How to Lead

- The person lying on the snow lifts the standing person until the arms are fully extended and then returns them to the snow.
- As a warmup, the drill should be done first without anyone standing on the hands; then do it with a light person, and then with a person of approximately the same weight.
- The standing person may help by making a jumping motion on a count of 3. Spotters could assist if the lifter has problems.
- The winner is the person who performs the most push-ups.

Safety Considerations

- Ensure that a spotter is used throughout this activity.
- Have another spotter standing behind the person to be lifted.

Back to Back

The object of this activity is to push an opponent over a marking on the snow (approximately 1 m).

Age or Grade Level

Any age or grade level

Number of Participants

Any number of participants; the activity is performed in pairs.

Equipment

None

Setup

- Mark a line approximately 3 feet (1 m) from the line on which participants are seated.
- Competitors sit back to back with one hand between their legs and the other to the side.

How to Lead

- On your "Go" signal, competitors use their feet, arms, and back to try to push the opponent backward across the line on the snow.
- Both hands and buttocks must remain in contact with the snow at all times, or the win is given to the opponent.
- To begin, have participants use their right arms to the side and their left in the middle. Have them perform the activity three times like this and then switch their arm positions. This will help them determine which arm they feel most comfortable with. However, competitors have to have the same arm to the side so as not to interfere with each other. If this becomes a problem, have participants choose partners who prefer the same-side arm in the middle (so that their arms are on opposite sides of each other).

- Have participants who are comfortable with the activity demonstrate it (one pair at a time) while the others watch. After the winner is declared, ask the observers why they think the winner was so effective. Discuss the role of the middle hand, the angle of the knees and back, the timing of the push, and the amount of grip between boots and snow.
- One defensive strategy is to plant both feet on the snow close to the buttocks.
- One offensive strategy is to shift one's weight to one side while the opponent is pushing to put the person off balance and set up for a counterpush.
- The winner is the person who wins two of three contests.

Safety Consideration

Ensure that participants are reasonably evenly matched.

Stick Pull

The object of this activity is to pull an opponent off the snow or pull a stick from his or her hands.

Age or Grade Level

Any age or grade level

Number of Participants

Any number of participants; the activity is done in pairs.

Equipment

For each pair, a broomstick about 16 inches (40 cm) long

Setup

- Competitors sit facing each other with knees bent and their soles touching. Both are holding the stick with two hands.
- One competitor has the inside grip (i.e., both hands inside the partner's hands).

How to Lead

- On a count of 3, competitors try to gain possession of the stick by using their arms and legs.
- On the second attempt, competitors switch their grips (the one with the inside grip uses an outside grip). In case of a tie, the winner of a coin toss or rock-paper-scissors gets to choose the grip.

- The winner is the person who wins two of three contests.
- Have a few pairs demonstrate this activity (one at a time) while the others watch. After the winner is declared, ask the observers why they think the winner was so effective. Discuss the role of the middle hands, the angle of the knees and back, and the timing of the pull.
- A good technique to use when the opponent pulls on the stick is to quickly extend the legs and back (i.e., produce more power from the legs).

Snow Fit Circuit

Once participants are familiar with the preceding native activities, you can set up an outdoor fitness circuit with stations.

Age or Grade Level

Any age or grade level

Number of Participants

Any number of participants

Equipment

Dependent on the activities selected

Setup

Select 6 to 10 activities, and divide participants into groups. Have each group select and set up an activity in an appropriately designated space.

How to Lead

- Participants are divided equally among the activity stations. In each of these groups, one participant should be chosen (by you or peers) to be the group leader; this leader ensures instructions are followed and the group moves together.
- Each group begins at a station, completes the activity, and on your cue moves (clockwise or counterclockwise) to the next station.
- If participants will be sweating, place this activity at the end of your outdoor session.
- In your activity debrief, focus on what participants gained through their participation in innovative games and activities in terms of understanding, appreciating, and valuing cultural identities and traditions.

Variation

You or your participants may select activities for the snow fit circuit.

Safety Consideration

The flow of activity stations should minimize the repetition of major muscle group use. In other words, when possible, plan the activity sequence to alternate between activities that focus primarily on upper- and lower-body muscle groups.

Snow Snake

Over 500 years ago, snow snake was used as a means of communication between tribes. As the communicative function diminished, the activity became competitive for some; for others, snow snake became an enjoyable pastime during the long winter. The snow snake is a wooden log with rounded edges that is thrown down a trough to see how far it will slide.

Age or Grade Level

Any age or grade level

Number of Participants

Any number of participants

Equipment

A piece of wood (or something similar) 6 inches to 6 feet (15 cm to 1.8 m) long, depending on the size trough you wish to build. Some tribes used bone for snow snakes. Be creative.

Setup

- Select your snow snakes before building the trough, because the trough must provide the snow snake minimal resistance and freedom to slide. Think of the trough as a bobsled or luge track.
- The trough should be approximately 5 inches (13 cm) deep and shaped to contain the snow snake.
- Mark the trough to indicate where to release the snow snake. Contact with the snow snake beyond this mark is a violation, nullifying the distance thrown, although it counts as a throw.

How to Lead

- Traditionally, there are two roles—the shiner, who takes care of and polishes the snow snake, and the thrower.
- Competitions occur between four teams, traditionally know as corners.
- Predetermine a set number of points to win (e.g., 10).
- In each round, each team makes four throws. The team making the longest throw is awarded 2 points; the team making the second-longest throw is awarded 1 point.

Variations

- Depending on the number of teams, play two teams against each other. Consider trying a snow snake ladder tournament in which teams can challenge others with the aim to get to and stay at the top of the ladder.
- Consider making all team members throwers.

Safety Consideration

Keep participants behind the thrower so that if the snow snake comes out of the trough, it will not strike anyone.

Igloo

The igloo is a quintessential icon of an outdoor life connected to the natural world, revealing an intimate understanding and dependency between people and nature.

Age or Grade Level

Any age or grade level, but more suited to older people

Number of Participants

Any number of participants

Equipment

Shovels; old handsaws and rectangular containers or buckets may also be helpful in making snow blocks.

Setup

Pack the snow that will be inside the igloo. To do so, four participants (or more, depending on the desired radius) stand shoulder to shoulder facing one direction. They walk forward like an airport spotlight, the person in the center staying in one place but moving to tether the others. This ensures that the radius is consistent, creating a relatively even circle.

How to Lead

- Cut the blocks as you go, because size and shape may change.
- Lay the first tier of blocks and fill any gaps.
- When laying the second tier of blocks, stagger the joints so the second-tier blocks cover the joints of the first-tier blocks below.
- Remember that each tier must come closer to the middle both vertically and horizontally. The supporting pressure is on the inner edges of the blocks, so make sure that these edges are in contact. Gaps between outside edges can be filled by hand packing loose snow into them.
- Continue to layer, using smaller blocks as you get higher.
- A larger thin block may be used to seal the top if the snow is suitable.
- Sleeping quarters in the igloo should be slightly above the entrance height to allow cooler air to descend and to have warmer air in the sleeping area.

Variation

A variation of the igloo is the quinzhee, in which snow is piled in an igloo shape, left for an hour so the snow crystals bond (or sinter), and then dug out so the walls and ceiling are 8 to 12 inches (20 to 30 cm) thick.

Safety Considerations

- Use caution when using cutting tools to make snow blocks.
- When building a quinzhee, dig in and up at the same time to avoid excessive snow load over the person inside the structure.

Trekking
Part III

Chapter 6

Snowshoeing

When considering winter activities for our program, snowshoeing is one of our first choices (if not the first choice). This is the result of two events that opened my eyes to the magic of snowshoes. The first was a personal winter camping experience over two decades ago. After a night of snow, the hike out was overly taxing. During a break, my hiking partner and I discussed the difficulty of predicting snowfall amounts. The forecast for our area had been very wrong: it called for 5 cm (2 in.) of snow, and we received 25 cm (10 in.). That difference changed our hike dramatically. As we repacked our water bottles and made the move to don our packs, I said, "You know what we need? Snowshoes!" We returned shortly after with snowshoes, and from that point on, the winter woods were wide open to us. What a difference they made.

The second event came after a snowshoeing session with a group of sixth-graders. We had spent the morning playing games and then done a short exploration of a greenbelt and wooded trail system that borders the school and neighboring community. While returning to the school, I was shoeing along with three of the stragglers, crossing the field to the back door of the building. As we approached the pile of snowshoes left by the kids who were now indoors changing, one little guy said, "Thanks, sir, I loved it. But you know what I like most about snowshoeing?" He paused, and I said, "Tell me what." "It's easy," he said. "I don't have to think about it—strap 'em on my feet and go, and I can keep up with everyone else and I can do what they're doing. For me, that's great! See ya." The stragglers were kids who were not on a school team, not typical athletes. Snowshoeing gave them an opportunity, with little technical background or skill, to get outside and have fun with everyone else. I understood then how simple it is to stay active—just strap 'em on your feet and go. The rest is up to me; I need to lead a positive winter outing. This chapter presents activities, tips, and shared experiences that will help you lead people outdoors on snowshoes so they can explore winter landscapes.

Getting Started

Ideally, we like to have the luxury of starting a group excursion at an established facility: a community center, school, or base camp. Shelter is helpful for getting participants organized, outfitted, and prepped to start some games. When introducing people to the pursuit of snowshoeing, the next requirement is a wide-open space with deep, fluffy snow. According to the age, fitness level, and interests of the participants, and the purpose of the program, we then choose warm-up activities, games, and a progression to build on if we are leading our group away from the base camp and into a wooded area—on trails or off.

Snowshoeing for Life

Snowshoeing is a great lifetime activity because it's simple and inexpensive enough for anyone to do, and it offers a great workout. It's excellent aerobic exercise that keeps bodies warm in the snow and burns calories, using every major muscle group at a relatively high intensity for extended periods of time. Snowshoeing can also build muscular strength and endurance!

If we are meeting a group at a trailhead, our plan is a bit different. We try to ensure that we have all paperwork (medical forms, permission forms) ahead of time, along with information on the group: ages, outdoor experience, and weight. Because some people are not comfortable sharing their weight, we ask for this in a tactful way (*Please provide information so that we can make the best snowshoe fit possible*). Getting information prior to the excursion is not always possible; when we are short on information, we make sure the program leans toward the conservative end of the risk-assessment continuum. A phone call is sometimes a good way to extract needed information. Teachers and after-school organizers can be great sources of inside knowledge of groups.

Prior to the group's arrival, we try to have all pieces of equipment laid out and ready for pickup. We organize our snowshoes by size to accommodate the variety of weights. This allows us to focus on and properly greet our participants in a positive way, with smiles, high-fives, eye contact, introductions—a general warm welcome that says "Glad you're here; we are excited about being outdoors with you."

After greetings and introductions, we point out piles of snowshoes based on size (small, medium, large, and extra large) and give weight ranges for each general size (e.g., if you weigh between 45 and 64 kg [100 and 140 lb], go to this pile), allowing participants to choose the size that will best support their weight. This is often referred to as *flotation*: the more flotation, the less you sink. But the bigger the snowshoe, the harder it is to manage. A GO leader needs to take the time to make the best fit for the maximum enjoyment. For people who are unsure of their weight, I use myself as an example: I tell them I am 91 kg (200 lb), and then I show them the size snowshoe I use. This provides a concrete reference. The important point is not to ask people to call out their weights; instead, give them the information they need to choose the appropriate size. Before moving on to attaching snowshoes to footwear, we ask participants to remember their snowshoe size for future reference.

Once participants have picked out their snowshoes, we move them to a fitting location, away from the cars and preferably not in the tree line. If shelter is available, we do this indoors. Regardless of where the fitting occurs, we break the group in half or into thirds and demonstrate the strapping technique. With smaller

Jon, in extra-large snowshoes, and Aaron, in medium snowshoes, exploring the backwoods of Kep-poch Mountain, Nova Scotia.
© Andrew Foran

first-time groups, you can do one-on-one coaching and enlist snowshoe veterans to help.

Each brand of snowshoe has its own binding system. Make sure you are famil-iar with the binding(s) of all the snowshoes you are providing. Modern snowshoes have lefts and rights, which may be stamped in the heel area. If not, make sure the binding buckles are on the outside of the foot so that the snowshoer doesn't clip them while striding, which can cause tripping. Eventually, a clipped buckle will break, presenting a field repair that is not simple.

Table 6.1 is a quick reference chart based on general snowshoe dimensions and average suggested weights.

Whether we are off-site or on-site, or whether we are leading a half-day or full-day trip, we always do a final gear check with the group. For extended excursions in which participants are expected to bring a substantial amount of equipment, we do the gear check after introductions and before fitting snowshoes. We want to make sure they have the essentials in their own packs, which can then be packed in a pulk or on a sled (more on that in just a bit). Our leader gear has already been sorted and checked and loaded into the pulk or sled. The important issue at this stage is to maximize activity and minimize standing around, shuffling papers, and getting cold.

TABLE 6.1   Snowshoe Sizing Guide

General size	Snowshoe dimensions in cm (in.)	Recommended weight range in kg (lb)
Small	51-56 (20-22)	45-64 (100-140)
Medium	64-66 (25-26)	64-82 (140-180)
Large	76-81 (30-32)	82-100 (180-220)
Extra large	89-91 (35-36)	100-127 (220-280)

Snowshoeing Equipment

As discussed in chapter 3, snowshoes fall into three categories that match the type of terrain for which they are best suited: beginner, intermediate, and advanced. Snowshoes also can be distinguished in terms of traditional or modern. The use of snowshoes to float over deep, powdery snow had its origins in First Nations ingenuity. The old wooden frames can be traced back to the time when these people were living closely with the land. (The different styles of wood-framed snowshoes had different purposes: wide, shorter bear paws were for powdery snow; the Algonquin wide, with its long, narrow heel, was for general trails; and the Alaskan was very long with a pointed toe and heel to move on crusty snow layers. In short, the people of the First Nations built their snowshoe to meet the winter conditions and terrain of their areas.) Technology has altered the appearance of the snowshoe now seen in the woods—from wooden frames to aluminum tubes, from the classic intricate sinew weave to a solid vinyl deck, from leather straps or lampwick bindings to webbed straps with ratcheting systems and cold-resistant rubber heel straps. All of these innovations have resulted in very durable and functional snowshoes for recreational users.

We have discovered that both traditional and modern snowshoe have advantages. The modern ones tend to be easier to care for, whereas the traditional ones require an annual varnishing and sealing before storage. The old-style bindings are easier to replace or repair than the click-and-flip ratchet-style bindings. The rubber straps on modern snowshoes, on the other hand, can be easily replaced—just remember to keep a few on hand. I find that the flotation of the more traditional shoe is better for me, but I am a stocky guy; the wider shoe gives me greater float and stability in powdery snow than the modern shoe does. However, I really appreciate the claw grips built into the underside of modern snowshoes. When the snow is crusty, these grips really help, and some shoes have a built-in heel lift to ease your hamstrings when tackling long ascents. To my surprise, when the bindings let go on my old Huron-style snowshoes, I was able to purchase a modern binding with rubber straps, a ratchet system, and a claw at the toe pivot—making my snowshoes a kind of crossover. These have become my new (old) favorites.

An important issue when choosing snowshoes for a program is practicality. The more strap adjustments there are and the more complex the binding system is, the harder it will be for youth (and any participants, really) to strap them on and go. If you can do a warm fit the day before or at least prior to heading out, encourage your participants to remember the numbers on their snowshoes (see the modern versions in the photo). This will save you setup time when you're out there. The simpler the binding is and the more that can be done with mittens on, the better.

Most important is knowing how to adjust or repair snowshoes on the fly. For example, heavy-duty electrical ties can be used to repair the bindings of modern snowshoes (e.g., to keep a ratchet in place). Electrical ties can also be used to secure the solid decking if a rivet lets go. For more substantial repairs, I always carry extra lengths of lampwick to make a new binding; this works for both modern and traditional-style shoes. These items are part of the field repair kit that is carried in the leader pack.

Figure 6.1 provides an overview of the components of a traditional snowshoe and a modern snowshoe.

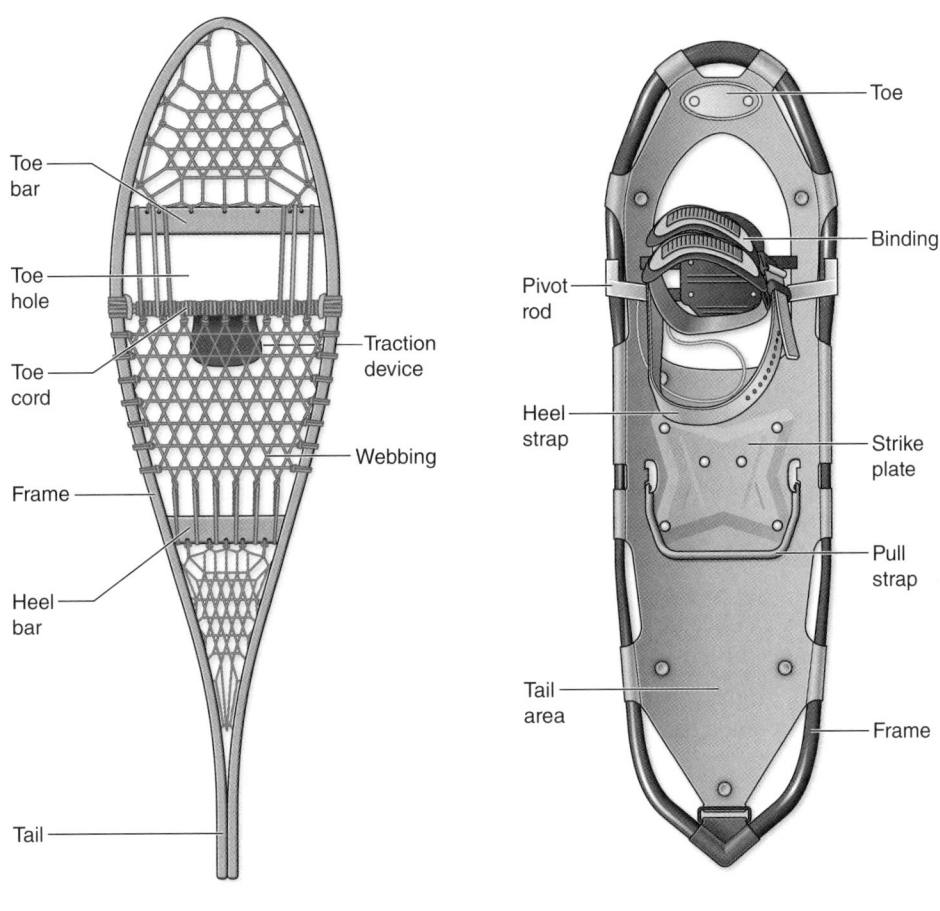

Traditional snowshoe **Modern snowshoe**

FIGURE 6.1 Parts of a snowshoe.

Snowshoeing Skills

Participants using traditional snowshoes need to learn how to stomp and stride. With traditional snowshoes we like to see as natural a gait as possible—that is, people walking normally, but with their feet just wide enough apart to prevent one snowshoe from impeding the other. This is necessary because traditional shoes are somewhat wider than modern shoes.

Modern snowshoes are sleeker, narrower, and lighter weight than traditional ones, which provides greater stability for some, especially those with small walking strides such as children. Not only does the lightweight material make the activity more accessible to many (if not all) age groups, but the design allows for a more natural stride. If your participants have modern snowshoes, remind them that they have a left and right shoe to prevent clipping and tripping when the buckles are on the insides of the feet. With modern shoes, participants can pretty much strap 'em on and go, although they may have to widen their stance a wee bit if they hear the click-click of tubing contact.

When I see that all group members are strapped into their snowshoes I ask them to stomp in a stationary spot to make sure the bindings are tight enough to get started. Next, have the group follow you to a spot on the field, and emphasize these actions:

- Widen your stance just enough to avoid stepping on the other snowshoe. This is more likely to happen with traditional shoes than with modern shoes.

- Traditional snowshoes tend to be wider and require a side-to-side motion, a flare in the gait, so that one snowshoe clears the other. Modern snowshoes are narrower and require less side-to-side motion.

- At the end of the stepping action, the heel of the snowshoe should touch the snow first. In fact, the heel of the snowshoe should drag slightly when the knee is lifted.

- In deep snow, a very slight press and pause at the end of each step allows the snow to compact under the snowshoe, providing more stability.

- If you are breaking a trail, keep your steps a little shorter and try to keep the tips—the toes of the snowshoe—from becoming loaded with snow. If the toe catches, it will trip you up. If the snow is crusty (this is really important), lift your knees and tilt your toes upward to clear the crust.

- Swaying slightly from side to side with each step and swinging your arms to create a more fluid hip motion might relieve some stress on the hip flexors.

- If the heel of the snowshoe lifts high or flicks up with each step, the back of your pants will be covered with snow, which may lead to wetness and discomfort. Remember to drag your heels.

- After a short distance, check for loose bindings. (Give them enough readjustment time; you may need to help younger snowshoers—mittens and bindings can present some challenges.)

Once participants have learned the shuffling gait for snowshoeing, the next skill is turning and staying balanced on the snow. The two types of turns are the step turn and the kick turn.

- The step turn involves stepping to the side one foot at a time to either change direction while walking or completely turn around (not so simple in traditional snowshoes, but easier in modern shoes). When turning right, the right foot steps first.
  - Take short, quick steps until you have turned.
  - The tail of the shoe covers very little distance; the toes move the most. The heel mostly drags behind the toe.
  - Really lift the knee and toe, because there will be snow buildup on the deck of modern snowshoes and you don't want them clipping the gutter (the depression made in the snow from their weight) or the toe getting hung up in the deep powder or crust.
  - Once you can balance well, practice sharp turns to the left and right.

- The kick turn is used for quick turns and changes of direction. It involves turning 180 degrees (i.e., turning on a dime). Make sure participants are spread out just a bit so they have room for arm movements and space to land if they fall.
  - When turning right, lift the right snowshoe and turn it clockwise so that the tip is next to the tail of the left snowshoe.
  - Picking up the left shoe, pivot the hips right so the left shoe is once again facing the same direction as the right shoe.

> ### *Ancient Snowshoeing*
>
> Snowshoes are one of the oldest forms of transportation. Archaeologists speculate that snowshoeing began 6,000 years ago in central Asia and that ancestors of the Inuit and Native Americans migrated to North America on snowshoes made from modified slabs of wood.

If coordination or balance is an issue for anyone, consider providing cross-country ski poles. The narrower the snowshoe is, the less stable the person will be when breaking trail, because the snow is shifting underneath. By the time the last person has followed in the gutter (the depression in the snow), the base underneath has become quite stable. Ski poles can help with balance while executing the kick turn. (*Note:* For safety reasons, do not allow ski poles to be used during game play.) A detailed overview of this skill progression is presented in *Quality Lesson Plans for Outdoor Education* (see reference list at end of chapter for full details).

Basic Snowshoeing Games and Activities

When choosing snowshoeing activities and games, consider cross-curricular connections, age appropriateness (most people like to play, but you need to be discerning—what activity will work best?), and modifications to meet the physical needs and interests of your participants as well as the environment. In short, any game that can be played on a field or in a gym can be played in the snow on snowshoes, with some modifications. Consider snow soccer, snow baseball, snow volleyball, snow ultimate, snow disc golf, hide and seek or capture the flag in the snow—you get the point. When that bank of games and activities runs its course, try a few of the following.

Pizza Tag

Introduce pizza tag once your participants are comfortable on their snowshoes. This game allows them to use their kick turns and step turns.

Age or Grade Level

Any age or grade level

Number of Participants

As many as you can get onto the snow

Equipment

Brightly colored pinny or funky hat to identify the tagger

Setup

- This game is best played on a patch of fresh, fluffy snow.
- Have participants follow you to make a circle that would accommodate every person standing with arms outstretched around the periphery. Make a couple of passes until the gutter is well packed down.
- Step outside the gutter and make another circle to double the width of the gutter. Again, make a couple of passes.
- Break a trail right through the middle of the circle.
- When you reach the gutter, turn left or right and follow it until you are halfway between the points of the cross-trail. Then turn into the circle again and break a trail across, cutting it in half (the circle is now divided into quarters).
- Continue until you have divided the circle into as many divisions as you can (it should look like a pizza).

How to Lead

- Explain that you are the chef and will try to tag players. Everyone must stay in the gutters—no hopping lanes, tackling, or passing.
- A tagged player becomes the chef—no tag-backs.
- This is not an elimination game—who wants to sit out in the cold?

Variations

In this game participants should be moving toward using the shuffling gait. If they have to turn in one of the narrow gutters, the kick turn should emerge. And as they stomp and stride along the circle (the outer crust), they should step turn into the pizza. Play a few rounds, mix up the chefs, or have a few chefs.

Safety Considerations

- Participants should now know how to tighten straps and adjust bindings and clothing, and this game will shake things loose. Younger players may need help with binding adjustments to stay in the game.
- Do not permit pushing, shoving, or tackling.
- Do not permit passing or jumping over other snowshoers; remember, there are sharp cleats on the bottoms of modern snowshoes.
- Provide breaks so that players can remove layers of clothing; they will heat up after a round or two.

Seeds

This is a game about food gathering as wild creatures and the challenges of securing enough food to survive.

Age or Grade Level

Because this game is somewhat complex, we suggest it for grades 3 and up.

Number of Participants

Try to have unequal teams: more juncos than jays, a few squirrels, and only a hawk or two.

Equipment

- One bucket for each player (coffee containers are great—reduce, reuse, recycle)
- Brightly colored ping-pong balls
- Markers to indicate the play zone
- Big bucket to serve as the big feeder (a pulk works great for this)

Setup

Find a wooded area with trees nicely spaced and deep snow. Mark the boundaries of the play zone using flagging tape or big orange pylons that are visible in the snow at a distance. Choose participants to be juncos, jays, and squirrels, and one hawk (there should be two jays for every eight juncos and one squirrel, and one hawk overall). Give each creature a bucket to serve as a nest, or home base. (We use empty Folgers coffee containers, which are red and very visible in the snow.) The object of the game is for creatures to gather as much food as possible to feed themselves and their young. Here are the steps for playing:

- Before beginning the game, assign someone to be the time caller. Nothing is more frustrating than having someone tell you the game is about to end when your strategy is beginning to gel!
- Each ping-pong ball represents one seed.
- Four seeds are enough to feed one baby.
- All creatures steal seeds from other creatures' nests.

How to Lead

- Play begins with all creatures at the feeder (the big bucket that hold the seeds).
- Give the creatures 50 seconds to hide their nests within the marked boundary, against trees and out of sight (no burying).
- All creatures then mull about the feeder, about 5 meters (16 ft) away, constantly moving until you say "Go."
- The juncos go first because they are the quickest. They swoop in and take no more than five seeds in one gloved or mittened hand—if they drop their seeds, well, that's squirrel food.
- When the last junco has left the feeder, the activity has alerted the jays, who seek out junco nests. If they find one, they can take three seeds. Jays may not return to the same nest consecutively.
- The juncos snowshoe to and from their nests, collecting food from the feeder.
- The squirrels can pick up as many seeds on the ground as they want and bring them to their nests. They may raid a junco nest, but the next nest they raid has to be a jay's, and from each nest they can take only two seeds. However, squirrels can run with as many seeds as they can—in their gloved or mittened hands.

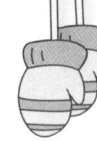

> ### Snow in Different Temperatures
>
> When it is extremely cold, snow takes a very fine powdery form and snowflakes appear simple in design, usually needle or rod shaped. When the temperature nears the freezing point (32 degrees Fahrenheit or 0 degrees Celsius), snowflakes become much larger and more complex in design.

- The hawk faces away from the action and, every 50 seconds, turns and runs toward the action. A hawk that grabs a creature has just scored lunch! The hawk takes the lunch to the end of the boundary area and returns after two minutes. A hawk that misses the prey must continue straight ahead to the end of the boundary and wait another 50 seconds before turning toward the action to try again.
- At the end of the determined time, "End" is called. At this point the creatures retrieve their nests and count how many young they were able to feed that day.

You may want to do a practice round before starting the game. Watch for emerging foraging strategies in the first round. Before the second and third rounds, allow creatures to rehide their nests—you will see some interesting ideas come out!

Variations

- For older participants (with bigger hands), use higher seed allowances.
- Add a few odd-colored ping-pong balls or golf balls to represent poison that causes illness in the nest.
- For large groups add a fox to hunt squirrels.

Safety Considerations

- Remind participants of the boundaries.
- Avoid densely treed areas.
- Issue safety glasses to protect eyes from low-lying branches.
- Remind participants about running and people awareness: no pushing or tackling to get to a seed!

Snow Script

This is a low-energy activity for slowing a group down. It can be used for debriefing a group experience and to allow for a bit of creative collaboration.

Age or Grade Level

Any age or grade level

Number of Participants

Any number of participants; the activity is usually done in groups of three.

Equipment

One spray bottle of colored water per group

Setup

A fresh patch of fluffy snow is best for this activity because people will be writing in the snow.

How to Lead

- Set up groups of three, and ask each group to answer a question about the experience, the session, the snowshoeing, or the adventure in one or two words.
- Groups then spread out and write their responses in the snow by stomping out letters.
- Bring all the groups in to the meeting zone when they have finished writing.
- All groups follow you to each word site (to keep people from unknowingly tromping through snow pages).
- At each snow page, participants try to read the snow word.

Variations

- To help the reading, give each group a spray bottle of colored water (food coloring) to trace their words in the snow. We typically do this only with younger participants, who usually like the coloring part of the activity.
- Reward points for the most letters or for obscure or sophisticated words.
- Present a limit that a snow phrase has to be used.

Safety Considerations

- Remind groups to find a snow page site within the marked boundary or designated area.
- Do not permit people to spray each other with the food coloring—wet and winter is not a fun mix.

Snow Art

This is a variation of snow script that can be done at a facility, school, or base camp with access to a large snow-covered field. You will be amazed at what people can draw (or stomp out) in the snow.

Age or Grade Level

Any age or grade level

Number of Participants

This can be a whole-group or small-group activity.

Equipment

None

Setup

- A large open field with fresh snow is best for this activity.
- Based on the number of participants, create two or three groups.
- Assign each group a large patch of fresh snow, removed from the other groups.

How to Lead

- The task is to stomp out a picture in the snow related to a predetermined theme (e.g., winter animals, popular summer activities, movie scenes—the choices are endless).
- Put a time limit on this activity; some groups have a real eye for snow art and become so engaged that you need to monitor when energy wans or they need a break.

Safety Consideration

Remind participants to strip down as they warm up; they will be working hard to fill their canvases!

Snow Hauling

This is a winter version of tug of war—with a few snowy considerations.

Age or Grade Level

This activity may appeal to older participants.

Number of Participants

Two teams

Equipment

Long piece of webbing 2.5 cm (1 in.) wide

Setup

- Find an open space at least 15 meters (50 ft) long with lots of fluffy, fresh snow.
- Stomp a line in the snow about midway, and position half the group on one side and the other half on the other side.

How to Lead

- Give each group an end of the piece of webbing.
- On your "Go," groups pull against each other until the last person in a group is pulled over the stomp line.

Variations

- For a twist, have the groups haul with the GO leaders. This variation is always a hit.

- If getting wet is not a concern, have the participants lie on their backs holding the webbing above their chests with their snowshoes in the air or in the snow. This variation requires a lot of energy, so save it for those high-energy groups.

Safety Consideration

Do not allow participants to wrap the webbing around hands or arms or any body part.

Freezer Burn Two-Group Challenge

This high-octane game has participants really running in snowshoes.

Age or Grade Level

Any age or grade level

Number of Participants

Any number of participants. I have played it with over 100 people without snowshoes, up to 40 with snowshoes.

Equipment

Rubber chicken or stuffed animal (with some weight—throwable!)

> ### *Feeling the Snowshoe Burn*
>
> Depending on intensity, snowshoeing can burn 400 to more than 1,000 calories per hour! Make sure your snowshoers are working at an intensity that keeps them warm without getting them drenched.

Setup

You need a large open space with lots of fluffy snow and two groups of snowshoers.

How to Lead

- Choose a game duration (e.g., five minutes). Rock-paper-scissors decides who goes first.
- Group A tosses the chicken, and group B chases it.
- When group B retrieves the chicken, members have to get into a straight line (reasonably, of course—they are on snowshoes) and then pass the chicken to the end of the line, going over the first person's head, then under the next person's legs, then over the next person's head, and so on. When the chicken reaches the end, the last person throws it as far from group A as possible.
- You may be wondering what the folks in group A are doing while group B is busy. Watching? Not likely. They are doing laps (well, one of them is). The group squeezes into a blob of snowshoers (it will look like some sort of abominable snowperson), and one person does as many laps as possible around the blob until group B chucks the chicken for them. Partial laps and laps completed after the chicken hits the snow do not count.

- Group A then has to shoe it to the chicken, get it off the snow quickly before it freezes (no feathers on a rubber chicken—hence the name, get it?), and then do what group B did.
- The process repeats until the time expires, at which point the group that completed the most laps has winner bragging rights.

Variation

Adjust the time to the energy level of the group.

Safety Considerations

- Remind participants to lift the toe of the snowshoe to prevent loading the front of the shoe with snow and tripping or catching the toe on a hard top layer of snow.
- Remind participants about people awareness.
- Make sure there are no buried obstructions that could cause injury—know your area!

Note: No group wants to lose its bragging rights to freezer burn, and everyone will be sweat soaked and exhausted and ready to go indoors after this game. For these reasons it should be the last activity of the day.

Knock 'Em Down, Get 'Em Up

This game is a classic GO Winter activity that has people practicing a lot of snowshoeing skills as they stoop, bend, reach, move, balance, and have fun.

Age or Grade Level

This game is a real hit with younger people, but university students have fun playing it too.

Number of Participants

As many as you can get onto the snow

Equipment

As many little pylons or field spots as there are people—or close anyway

Setup

- Set up a boundary on slightly tromped snow (this prevents losing field markers).
- Set up half the pylons standing and the other half on their sides, or half the field spots upright and the other half flipped over.

How to Lead

- Split the group in half. One half is the stand-'em-up crew; they want to put things right by having all the pylons and field spots upright. The other half is the knock-'em-down crew; they want to knock things down to make things right. Explain to participants that both groups are good; they just want different things.

- Pylons or field markers cannot be moved, just knocked down or set upright. Make sure everyone understands what *knock-'em-down* means (this can be confusing with field spots).
- Players may not guard the pylons or field spots.
- Players may not kick the pylons or field spots.

Variation

Set a time limit.

Safety Consideration

Players may not push, shove, tackle, or jump over other players.

Nice to Meet You—Making Tree Friends

This is a classic environmental game: fun in the summer and just as fun in the winter. The key learning (beyond moving on snowshoes) is trusting a partner and identifying the trees in the area.

Age or Grade Level

Any age or grade level

Number of Participants

Any number of participants; this activity is done in pairs.

Equipment

- Blindfolds, one per pair
- Laminated pictures of trees

Hoarfrost

When ice crystals fall on a surface such as tree branches, leaves, or wires that is lower in temperature (below freezing) than the surrounding atmosphere, the result is the rapid freezing of the moist crystals into solid state. This is known as hoarfrost, and it can make for surreal and beautiful scenes.

Setup

- Choose a forested area.
- Set participants up in pairs, and give each pair a blindfold. Do a group check before the activity to see if anyone is uncomfortable wearing a blindfold. Those who are can be spotters.

How to Lead

- The sighted snowshoer brings the partner to an interesting tree and makes an introduction.
- The blindfolded partner may touch the tree for about two minutes.
- The sighted snowshoer then leads the partner back to the starting point.
- The blindfolded snowshoer removes the blindfold and tries to find the tree. (The partner can give hints—"cold, colder"—if needed.) Once the trees are found, everyone returns to the starting point, and partners switch roles.

- It is helpful to do this activity after you have been in an area for a bit so there are tracks already in the snow. If you do it as soon as you arrive in a wooded area, the game becomes tracker—a fun game, but different.

Variation: Tree Identification

Tree identification in spring and summer is a bit easier than in winter because leaves really help to narrow things down. For this activity, we break the group into three crews. Here are the directions:

- Give each group several laminated pictures of trees—at least six (more if you have the budget). Tie them together at the top with a piece of twine (staples don't hold up). Make sure pictures show the bark well.
- Decide on a time frame based on participants' ability to focus (e.g., five minutes), and then send them out to identify as many trees as they can.
- At the end of the time, have them report in and take you to at least one tree they were 100 percent positive about, one they were mixed on, and one they just did not know. By the time all the groups have introduced you to the trees, you will be surprised at how many they could identify in winter, without leaves!

Safety Considerations

- Remind sighted partners of the boundaries and to be safe, trustworthy leaders.
- Do not allow people to lead partners into overly challenging areas.
- Do not allow sighted partners to abandon blindfolded partners.

The Cache

This activity could be a treasure hunt or a code-breaking challenge—you decide. Either way, with some prior setup, this will become a winter classic.

Age or Grade Level

Because of the technical requirements, and the time needed to teach how to use a GPS unit, you may want to limit this activity to older participants.

Number of Participants

Any number of participants in groups of two or three (maximum) per GPS unit

Equipment

- GPS units (one per group of two or three people)
- Buckets (see the seeds game for ideas)
- Code to decipher
- Extra batteries (remember, the winter cold will sap battery power quickly)

Setup

- Decide what you want participants to find.
- Clear your GPS units, check their battery life, and begin setting up the caches or hiding them in advance.

- For younger groups, preset the waypoints as 001, 002, 003, and so on, to correspond with the number of caches.
- For older participants, plugging in coordinates is a good thing to learn.
- You may want to review the Skills for Hills section later in this chapter if your geocache route takes participants into hilly terrain.
- When setting up your caches in advance, you don't want your tracks to lead participants right to them. To avoid this, you can come at the hiding spots from a different direction than they will, or set them up prior to a snowfall that will cover your tracks.
- Make sure the hiding place is a bit elevated or protected so that the caches don't become buried in snow. If they do become somewhat covered, red containers can help (again, large Folgers coffee cans work well).
- Provide excellent hints for finding the caches.
- Take some time to devise a thoughtful code that needs to be cracked. For example, each cache can contain a letter, all of which spell a winter-related word—now there's a chilly thought!

How to Lead

Send each group out with a GPS unit to begin the hunt.

Variations

- Use different types of containers to ramp up the challenge.
- Introduce a time constraint: as many finds as possible within a time limit.
- Have each cache contain numbers; the groups must share their discovered numbers and compile the findings to get the coordinates for the next cache, which the entire group hunts down.

Safety Considerations

- Ensure that boundaries are clearly marked to prevent groups from wandering off.
- Make sure the cache area has well-defined boundaries to prevent groups from getting lost as a result of human error or technical failure.
- At times, groups may not be visible. This is an opportunity to have older participants serve as GO assistants.

Ultimate Challenge Course (UCC)

This activity fosters imagination and provides a challenge. Be creative and work with what you have; this is about making junk worthwhile. And because it's junk, you don't have to worry about leaving it out between groups.

Age or Grade Level

All ages can play, but the design needs to be age appropriate.

Number of Participants

Any number of participants; this can be a large-group or small-group activity

Equipment

- Lots of stuff!
- Pylons
- Plastic flexible tubing 2.5 cm (1 in.) in diameter
- Hula hoops
- Piles of snow
- Logs 122 cm (4 ft) in length
- Plastic sonotubes for tunnels, 91.4 cm (3 ft) or 122 cm (4 ft) in diameter and whatever length you can get (at least 2 m is good)
- Old tires

Setup

This activity is basically a giant obstacle course to be completed on snowshoes. One sample course layout is shown in figure 6.2, but that's just one of a million possibilities; let your imagination run wild! We like to start the group outside and away from the UCC, preferably in front of a large snowbank, such as those at the edges of parking lots. We make sure the participants move toward the UCC and not toward the parking area—and leave a GO leader to monitor this area.

How to Lead

Following is a suggestion for a bare-bones UCC. Use your imagination to make use of items at your disposal.

- Participants climb the large (parking lot) snowbank without snowshoes, slide down the other side, and run about 15 m to the UCC entrance.
- When they arrive, they are blindfold by a GO leader. They then make their way to the snowshoe pile (a random mix) and strap a pair to their feet (this pile is about 15 m from the entrance).
- They then snowshoe run back to the GO leader, return the blindfold, and run to the up-and-down portion: pylons are cemented into the snow with a plastic tubing stuck in the top to make archways they must go through.
- They jump over the next pile of snow (running jumps are encouraged).
- They then roll into and out of a trench.
- The next challenge is foxholes. Participants start in the first foxhole, lift one leg, twist, and plant it in the next hole; they do the same with the second leg, continuing until all the foxholes are cleared.
- At the tire station, participants roll or carry a medium-size truck tire across the snow and swap it with a large truck tire that they must bring back—either rolling or carrying.
- Next are at least two tunnels to crawl through.
- At the island hop, participants hop from hula hoop to hula hoop until they reach a sled.
- With the sled, participants haul a GO leader back to the entrance of the UCC.

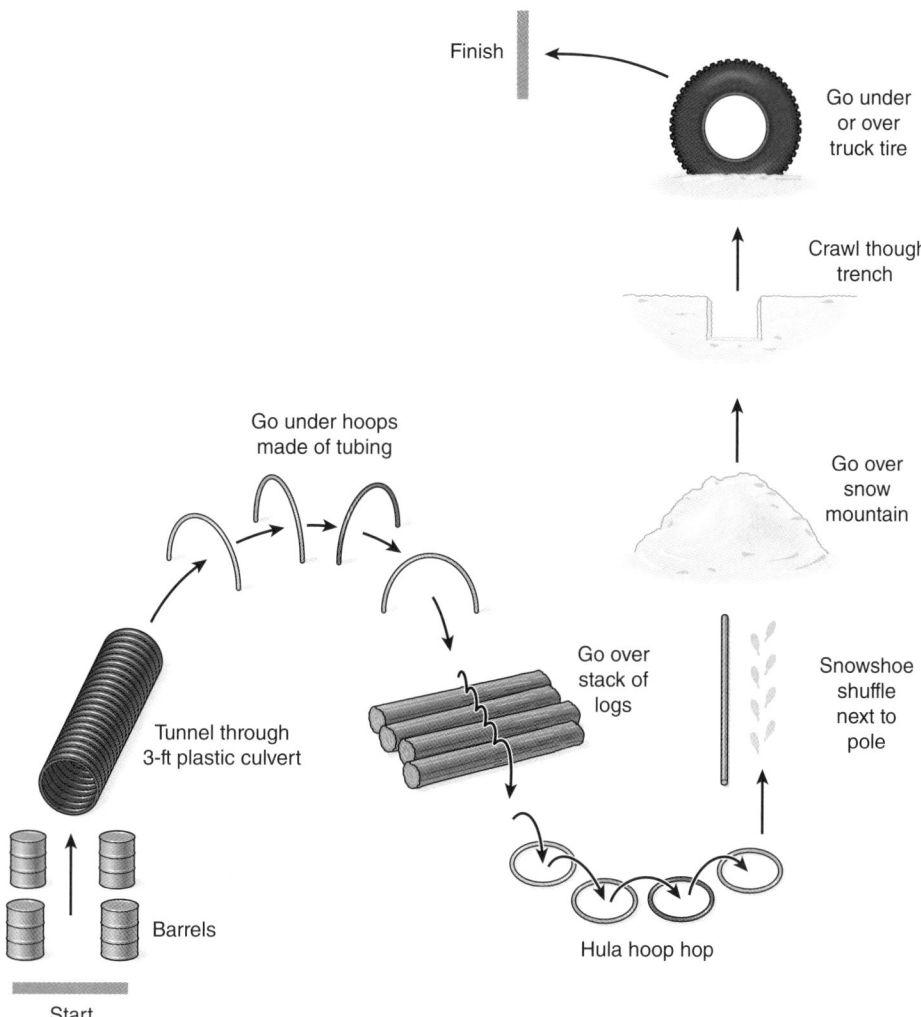

FIGURE 6.2   A suggested layout for an ultimate challenge course.

Variations

- Mix and match the obstacles —this is about imagination!
- Participants who are not comfortable wearing a blindfold can spot at locations along the UCC.

Safety Consideration

- Make sure the challenge is age appropriate and matches participants' physical abilities. Remember, this is not boot camp or a preschool for a Navy Seals winter brigade.

Skills for Hills

One of the best things about snowshoeing is that you can get off the beaten track to explore woodland terrain. Navigation skills are essential if you are leading groups in areas that are not contained like municipal parks. You need to know the natural boundaries, geographic benchmarks, where to go next, and how to arrive back at your starting point. Relying on following your tracks back may not work if you cross other tracks made by a different party going in a different direction. This has happened! If you are snowshoeing during a snowfall, it's amazing how quickly tracks can get covered.

Every route provides opportunities for exploration and adventure; you may encounter obstacles, waterways, and hills—which is great. However, features you see on a map may not be evident on the ground because of snow cover. Therefore, knowing the area is a must. With your leadership team, decide whether you have the skills yourselves to lead groups in a particular area. You must also determine whether the group you plan to lead has the skills to explore the area you are considering. For the most part, try to keep things reasonable; moderate hills are often more than enough to provide the adventure you want. With that said, if you will be encountering hills, your participants will need some instruction on ascending and descending in snowshoes.

Modern snowshoes have built-in crampons, metal claws at the toe and a metal cleat under the decking to help with climbing. This is particularly helpful on packed, icy, or crusty snow. On descents, these claws provide some grip during the slip caused by a combination of gravity and loose snow. Traditional snowshoes, which don't normally have metal cleats and toe claws (except for the hybrid bindings discussed earlier), require some strategies when ascending and descending.

Ascending

Start small, on gradual slopes, until participants are comfortable moving uphill in shifting snow. The key to ascending is short steps. Encourage participants using modern snowshoes to dig their toes in with each step; doing so creates a bit of pack and helps with traction. Digging in prevents the planted foot from slipping backward, resulting in a lost stride and falling forward into the snow. Explain that it is like building snow steps; the people who follow improve on the effort with continual snow packing.

On a moderate slope, the technique is the same, unless the slope is too steep or covered in powdery snow. In this case, participants should use the herringbone step, which involves widening the stance slightly (to hip width, if comfortable) and turning the toes out (the gait is now flared) so that more of the snowshoe is placed horizontally. This provides a wider base of support than the person would have trying to walk straight up the hill with vertical strides. With the herringbone step, encourage a slight forward lean to help shift the weight toward the goal, rather than standing upright, which can shift the weight back down the hill.

Herringbone step.
© Andrew Foran

If balance and timing are contributing to slipping (i.e., staying perched on the toes too long causes a slip), demonstrate the ascending technique of edging, as follows:

- Step with the lead (i.e., uphill) foot, and press into the snow to achieve a base for support. Bring the second foot up just below the lead foot and also press it into the snow. This needs to occur in an upward hopping motion. Now that the downslope snowshoe is on the snow platform created by the upslope snowshoe, repeat the action again and again.
- If you are getting tired as a result of the pressure on the upslope leg while hopping and stomping, switch lead legs by performing a kick turn on the hillside. With a new lead leg, repeat, repeat, repeat, until you are at the top.

When the snow cover is dry and loose, edging will be frustrating because of the constant downward slide on the hop. In this situation, switchbacks can help.

- In short, a switchback is a zigzag walk, back and forth across a hill, using the skills of edging and turning. Never going straight up, participants are always angled to the slope of the hillside.

- Participants will figure out that switchbacking means more snowshoeing because of the increased distance, but it is not as exhausting as climbing straight up. They will thank you for it.

- When turning left or right on the slope (angled upward, of course), people have to use the kick turn to maintain the angle and avoid going straight up the hill. This must be done efficiently, or they may slide downward a bit (or a lot) as a result of the quality of the snowpack.

Even the most experienced snowshoer cannot use the herringbone step indefinitely; this technique exhausts the hip flexors and thigh muscles. Consider providing cross-country ski poles or hiking poles to give snowshoers perch. Every bit of digging action helps get them up the hill. If you are using the switchback or going straight up, don't forget to engage the heel lifts if your modern snowshoes have them. This nice little device saves a lot of energy.

If participants are experienced and fit people who are ready for more snow challenges, consider expanding the route to include steeper inclines. To maintain upward momentum using the herringbone step, people can hunch over to grope the snow with their hands. Here are the steps:

Groping.
© Andrew Foran

- Bend at the knees and waist until your hands are on the ground between your snowshoes.
- Turn the toes of your snowshoes out in a herringbone technique.
- Dig your hands into the snow to assist in getting up the hill.

These techniques are all well and good with modern snowshoes, but what if your participants (and you) are wearing traditional snowshoes? Well, you do what seasoned snowshoers call toeing-out, as follows:

- Loosen the bindings on the shoes so the toes of your boots poke through the toe hole.
- Snowshoe straight up the hill with the toes of your boots poking through and sticking into the snowbank. Drive these toes right into the bank of snow—kick inward and pack the snow.
- Groping helps too; use those hands and dig your way upward!

Toeing is not simple and requires practice on moderate slopes until the technique is mastered and confidence is gained. Another option available to traditional snowshoers climbing a hill is taking off one snowshoe and using it as a pole assist, as follows:

- Lock the tail of the snowshoe into the snow before applying weight to the modified pole.
- Do not expect to make huge bounds upward; think in terms of micro advances, and maintain a comfortable reach to prevent downward slipping. If you overextend, you slip down more than you go up.
- When you are ready to replant the snowshoe upslope, lift it out of the snow quickly, move upward, and position your weight over the top of the snowshoe by hanging on to the toe.

When using a snowshoe as a modified pole, avoid jamming or thrusting it, or overextending your upward reach. Jamming the tail of the snowshoe into hard snowpack or the ground may break the snowshoe; moreover, doing so is overly exhausting with minimal upward gain for the output of effort.

Note: Steep slopes pose avalanche risks, which are discussed minimally in chapter 8, Winter Camping. We recommend avoiding avalanche areas entirely; avalanche safety is well outside the scope of this book.

Descending

Life is not all uphill, despite what our parents might have said about their childhood journeys walking to school in rain and snow. What goes up must come down. This section provides some options for descending hills safely, preventing the downhill ski method that usually results in disaster. Skiing on snowshoes is not a skill!

Choose an area with slopes of varying degrees of steepness for practicing descents. Descending, like ascending, can be done progressively based on participants' fitness level, skills, and readiness to take on the challenge.

Descending a hill.
© Andrew Foran

For mild slopes, people should lean slightly backward and position their body weight somewhat over the back deck or the tail of the snowshoe. Leaning too far back will result in a fall, so this is about maintaining balance while moving, and that's a skill! Encourage your participants to do the following:

- Take short, quick steps to avoid tripping in deep snow.
- Think of the steps as trying to pack down deep snow or push excess snow down the hillside, using the buildup of powder as a natural brake.
- If the momentum picks up to a pace quicker than you'd like, sit and use your bum as a human brake!

If your group is bum-breaking the whole way down, you may want to try another option. From your leader pack, provide each participant with two pieces of rope or webbing. Then present these instructions:

- Tie a piece of rope or webbing through the top of each snowshoe, through the weave and around the frame, or past the solid deck and around the frame.
- Grasp the rope or webbing with the corresponding hand, and wrap it as needed around your hand to take up any excessive length to prevent getting tangled up.

- Pulling on the rope or webbing prevents the toe of the snowshoe from going under the snow crust or becoming trapped under the snow and causing a forward fall that is pointing downhill.
- While moving down the hill, pull the shoe slightly by tugging on the webbing to elevate the toe, dig in the heel, and increase the angle to push more snow out in front of you. Lean back as much as you can—a comfortable lean!

As soon as they feel the sweet spot (backward learn, upward pull, downward momentum), participants will love this form of descent. And remember, anytime they don't like the momentum, they should remember the human braking system—the bum!

Not all hills will be moderate or mild; you will encounter steep slopes. Also, you will want to build in a few physical challenges as the group gains confidence. We have found that the safest way to tackle steep descents for most snowshoers is to use the edging technique, as follows:

- At the top of the hill, turn sideways.
- Using your lower leg, stomp repeatedly with your snowshoe to create a packed snow ledge—don't rush this.
- When the ledge is well packed, hop up slightly, lifting the snowshoes off the snow. Time the landing so the upslope snowshoe lands on the platform and the downslope snowshoe lands in fresh snow ready for pounding.
- Repeat this downward step-building process until you arrive at a more moderate slope or you reach the bottom.
- The edging technique can be coupled with the switchback technique.
- If your platform gives way and you start body surfing on the snow, lean back until your entire body is in contact with the snow, spread your arms out, flap them downward, dig into the snow to slow yourself down, and use your feet, legs slightly spread, to kick downward and dig into the snow.

You need to exercise caution on extremely steep hills. Claws or no claws, gravity and snow can send you all careening downward. Encourage your participants to maintain a backward lean on steep descents in case they lose their balance in shifting snow. Falling backward into powder is better than falling forward into a face plant or tumbling head over heels to the bottom!

Remind your participants of the safety considerations for ascents and descents. Also, pick slopes that match your participants' abilities. Regardless of how well a group is doing, however, some slopes should be avoided. Overhangs should be avoided because of the risk of an avalanche. Even a small avalanche can be a disaster, so if you are unsure, have your participants track around the hill.

Always review snow conditions and consider your limits to ensure personal and group safety. Hills can be fun—and they can also teach hard lessons in human gravity! Visit hill sites, examine slopes with participants, select techniques, and be able to explain why you are deciding to skirt a slope for the sake of safety. Deep snow can mask steep depressions and drops, which is why it's important to know the hilly area before bringing in a group. Deep, powdery snow is difficult to climb, offers a fantastic workout, and can be a lot of fun to descend. Crusty and hard-packed snow, on the other hand, is easier to climb as long as the necessary traction can be attained.

Advanced Snowshoeing Games and Activities

Once your group can handle ascending and descending on snowshoes, you can lead them in activities that require these skills.

Tapping Trees

Now that your participants can identify some trees, and they have learned some essential skills for hills, you can take them into a wooded area in search of maple or birch trees to tap.

Age or Grade Level

Any age or grade level

Number of Participants

Any number of participants—small or large group

Equipment

- Spouts
- Buckets
- Wire
- Hand drill
- Appropriate-size bit
- Flagging tape
- Hammer or rubber mallet
- Large pot, stove, and fuel

Setup

This late winter (in some places, early spring) activity is a most enjoyable experience for many people of all ages. The time to tap maple trees is when the daytime temperature rises above freezing, allowing the sap to run, and the nighttime temperature drops below freezing, sending the sap back down into the roots. This small seasonal window can provide a rich and tasty adventure. With a little background research, and from talking with locals, you may discover tips and modifications to shape this activity for your geographic area.

How to Lead

- This activity has to be spread over two or three days, so you may need additional activities to draw on until the sap fills your buckets.
- Mark trees for tapping with flagging tape for easy checking the next day. Number the tape strands and buckets to ensure that you check them all and retrieve them all at the end of the activity.
- Tap each selected tree with the hand drill. When you reach the desired depth (past the bark), gently hammer in the spout and hang the bucket.
- We encourage the use of used 1-liter pop bottles and 4-liter milk jugs. With a little ingenuity, these can be modified to hang off your tap and secured with a bit of bailing wire.

Sap bucket.
Photo courtesy of Greg Lukeman

- Give the trees 24 hours to fill their buckets with sap. Be patient; this might take a couple of days. Be prepared to boil on the second day, just in case.
- Boiling is not a fast process, but it's worth it. Remember, the boil needs to be watched to ensure you do not overboil and ruin the consistency.
- Once the sap has boiled down to syrup, you can make snow candy—a perfect winter treat—by pouring the syrup onto a clean bed of snow, allowing it to harden, and then scooping it off the snow with a stick.
- Ten liters of sap will make 1 liter of syrup.

Variations

- Instead of maple trees, you can tap birch trees.
- Instead of making maple syrup, do some research and consider making chaga tea—a wonderful winter treat.

Safety Considerations

- Make a reasonable route plan with realistic snowshoeing limits when scouting trees.
- Follow a group management procedure to keep the group together during the flagging and collecting.
- Be mindful of the terrain and hidden waterways when scouting for trees.

Snow Dancer

This activity makes a great warm-up or group refocuser. As your group begins to learn your ways, you can signal to them that a dance is about to happen. One of the GO leaders can begin to clap a rhythm to a recognizable song. (Not everyone has this skill, so practice beforehand and test your efforts with family and friends.) Once you have the group's attention, gather them in a circle, arm's length apart, and start some fancy footwork to match the beat of the song.

Snow dancing leaders should be able to move to the beat, not dance necessarily. This is about getting participants moving and having fun! Funky is allowed, expression is encouraged, and freedom is the order of the day. When you have all GO participants moving and it resembles a dance of sorts—success! Some dances we have tried and had fun with are the waltz, line dancing, break dancing, folk dancing, and disco dancing. All you really need to make this work is snow and people.

Variation

Turn the dance leading over to two or three participants; inform them that they will need to be ready at some point in the session or the next day. You will be amazed at how complex and synchronized these snow dances can become.

Snow dancing.
© Kevin Redmond

Running in Snowshoes

You may want your group to run or jog or trot at some point on a snowshoe outing. We are not talking about a marathon or Ironman training; this is about fun and challenging GO participants to get their knees up and their arms pumping. We teach snowshoe running just for technique; then we move our groups into a series of games. Otherwise, running becomes a taxing exercise. After a few falls (and there will be a few), exhaustion will set in.

Here are some tips for helping your group grasp the technique of snowshoe running:

- Start off slow—think technique first, then speed.
- The progression should be slow to avoid falls from the start—they will need to save their energy.
- Snow topped with a layer of crust makes running difficult because the tip of the snowshoe can hook underneath the crusty layer and cause a stumble or fall onto hard layers of snow. Beware of this.
- First attempts at running should be on well-packed surfaces to avoid hooking up in deep snow.

Running in snowshoes.
© Andrew Foran

Running in snowshoes is not just fast walking. Deliberate movements are required to allow the speed of the gait to maximize the distance of the stride. Speed is determined by snow depth and the unique ability of each participant to move quickly over the snow. Speed on snow depends on how far the person sinks into the powder, how high the snowshoe is lifted to clear the snow surface, and how well the toes of the snowshoes clear the edge of the snowshoe depression (the footprint in the snow). How fast people can go is an extension of their running gait. Stress the following:

- Arm action is crucial; a full pumping action, with arms opposite feet, encourages the legs to stride fully.
- The heel should strike first as in regular running.
- The height of the knee lift depends on the depth of the snow; deep snow requires higher knee lift to clear the surface.
- To be efficient, the knee lift should be just high enough to clear the surface of the snow.
- Striding should be as natural as running on dry land.
- Deep snow running can be very fun, but very strenuous. It's all about getting the snowshoe out of the snow quickly—keep those toes up!

Snow Train

This activity is a leg burner. In this snow train, the sled is the caboose, the participants are the cargo, and the runner is the engine. Everyone will have a chance to be the engine.

Age or Grade Level

Any age or grade level, although it is a favorite with younger participants.

Number of Participants

Any number of participants—the more the merrier.

Equipment

- One sled per team
- Loops of webbing 244-305 cm (8-10 ft) in length
- Pylons to mark a start and end zone

Setup

- Divide the group into teams (one team per sled).
- Using the sleds and the webbing, each team makes a train, and one snowshoer is the engine.

How to Lead

- Once a team has crossed the designated distance, a different participant becomes the engine for the next lap. This is repeated until everyone has had a chance to be the engine.
- The winners are the teams that have enough strength left to cross the finish line.
- We promise that they will be tired after this one.

Variations

Build in a few team tasks at the end of each lap that must be accomplished before the next round.

Safety Considerations

- Keep the weight factor and distance reasonable.
- Do not do this in hilly areas or include slopes!

Reference

Redmond, K., Foran, A., Dwyer, S. (2010). *Quality lesson plans for outdoor education*. Champaign, IL: Human Kinetics.

Chapter 7
Nordic Skiing

Nordic skiing is a satisfying, invigorating form of exercise that provides a great workout while minimizing impact to the joints. In most cases, Nordic skiing occurs along extended groomed trails and loops, which provides a sense of progress and makes it more interesting than repetitive exercises in limited space. The cooler temperatures of winter encourage continuous movement and activity. Nordic skiing is equally suited to the groomed trails of a well-developed ski park, the ungroomed terrain surrounding a school or community center, or a wilderness area or park. For all of these reasons and more, Nordic skiing is one of the best aerobic activities available. Competitive Nordic skiers have the highest recorded aerobic capacity of all athletes. Part of what makes the sport such a workout is the vigorous arm movements that accompany the leg movements. Arm activity elicits a higher heart rate than leg movement because blood has to be pumped against gravity.

This chapter presents a variety of skiing activities as well as information about how to prepare for them. First, let's look at the two styles of Nordic skiing (classic and skate)—how they evolved, how they differ from each other, and how to fit people for each.

Nordic Ski Equipment

Like snowshoeing, Nordic skiing began as a slow but practical way to travel on top of snow. Nordic skiing in Scandinavia dates back about 4,500 years. In early skis the boot toe was bound to the ski and a free heel permitting the foot behind the ball to move up and down according to the conditions and technique. Alpine skiing evolved to using a fixed toe and heel binding, while Nordic skiing maintained the free heel. Ski materials have evolved from wood, fiberglass, and Kevlar to modern composites. Although the science of ski waxing is essential to ski racers, the advent of the waxless Nordic ski minimizes the need to wax, offering a friendly starting point for beginner skiers.

Nordic ski bindings have evolved from a three-pin toe clip to a variety of modern bindings that ensure a fixed toe while guiding the boot into a track for each stride and glide. Nordic ski boots have evolved along with bindings. With the wide variety of bindings available, it is important to ensure that boot and binding match so they attach properly.

Up until the early 1980s, the primary technique in Nordic skiing was the diagonal stride commonly referred to as the classic technique. The traditional *classic* diagonal stride and glide technique uses some form of grip (under the middle third of the ski) for traction followed by a glide on the front and tail of the ski. This technique is then repeated on the opposite ski. An arm propulsion occurs opposite the glide ski. This classic style is the easier technique to learn. Beginner skiers can usually maintain a desired tempo and travel the preferred distance at their own pace. Early beginners often get along at a shuffle, whereas more experienced skiers develop the stride and glide technique that offers some recovery in the glide phase that follows each propulsive movement.

The second common ski technique is skating. This style grew in popularity in the early 1980s, when competitive skiers found that they could go much faster by waxing their skis for glide only and using a skating technique aided with pole propulsion. The technique appears very easy and fast, but it requires a lot of effort, high fitness levels, and good technique. For this reason most leaders introduce the classic style before the skate style. (For more information about fundamental skiing skills and the instructional progressions for classic and skate skiing, see *Quality Lesson Plans for Outdoor Education, published by Human Kinetics.*) If you have young participants who are fit and keen, they may be receptive to an early introduction to the skate technique. With such a group, be sure to intermix activities with regular rest intervals for partial recovery, but don't let them become too cold while resting.

In summary, classic Nordic skiing features a diagonal stride and glide, whereas the skate technique requires waxing for glide only and sufficient momentum to glide forward with each step. Although the skate technique appears faster and relatively effortless, it requires intense effort, especially when ascending. Between the skate and classic ski styles, there is something for everyone. Participants will also discover that different temperatures and snow conditions influence the grip, glide, and efficiency of both their skis and their skiing style.

This chapter does not provide detail guidelines for purchasing ski equipment because most program participants use institutional or rental equipment. You

a   b

Classic ski, boot, and binding *(a)*; skate ski, boot, and binding *(b)*.
©Kevin Redmond

do need to understand how equipment is sized to maximize comfort, efficiency, and success. Following are some guidelines for choosing appropriately sized equipment:

- Classic poles should measure from the ground to the armpit (for touring or beginners) or to the collarbone (for a more vigorous workout).
- Classic skis should measure 110 to 120 percent of the person's height. Also check for body weight. (Many ski manufacturers provide a skier weight range for each length of ski they sell.)
- Skate poles should measure from the ground to the chin or lower lip.
- Skate skis should measure 106 to 110 percent of the person's height, to a maximum of ~197 cm.

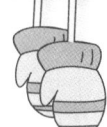

Wood You Like to Ski?

The word "ski" comes from the Norwegian word for "wood." A tribe in China still makes skis using split spruce trees and wrapping dried horse skin around them for friction.

Dressing for Skiing

Comfort and function are the objectives when dressing for any style of skiing. The purpose of ski clothing is to avoid temperature extremes (i.e., getting too hot or too cold). The guidelines in this section are not one size fits all. Young children, for example, have a lower percentage of body fat and higher metabolism than adults and older children and thus can become chilled faster. For this reason, for young children, add one medium-weight midlayer to the suggestions in this discussion.

Depending on the degree of exertion, not much clothing is required for Nordic skiing, even in relatively cool temperatures. For example, in a temperature range of 3 to –12 °C (37 to 10 °F), a light long sleeve wool top under a wind-breaking ski shell with a lighter material in the back is ideal. The wool top wicks moisture away from the skin and also insulates, providing warmth, while the back of the shell vents excess heat and moisture. The limitation of this system is noticeable when you stop for an extended time—you are prone to chilling quickly.

Beginners should layer up so they begin comfortable and can strip down as required. After two or three sessions, participants will know what layers work best. I choose my clothing based on the wind, sun, and temperature; I like to start out comfortable to comfortably cool. Within a few minutes of skiing, I'm warm.

Many skiers wear single-layer pants, often with a wind block layer in the front. Some add a base layer to wick moisture and, in very cold conditions, a midlayer for warmth. For the temperatures listed earlier, single-layer pants that prevent wind from blowing through the front are suitable for the average adult.

A light glove shell is suitable for people whose hands stay warm when they are active. Light or medium-weight merino wool glove liners covered by a wind-breaking shell are appropriate for those who need an added layer to keep their fingers warm.

A windproof, breathable hat is suitable for hard skiing in cool temperatures or easy skiing in milder conditions. A midlayer wool hat is best for easy skiing in vigorous conditions.

When it comes to socks, cotton kills, wool thrills! A medium-weight wool (e.g., Smartwool or merino) sock is recommended. Avoid thick or heavy socks that make ski boots tight because this can limit circulation and increase cooling.

Nordic ski boots should fit snugly; they should never be tight or loose. Tight boots reduce blood circulation and lead to cold feet and an increased risk of frostbite. Boots that are too loose increase the risk of blisters. We recommend that skiers carry a second pair of socks when being fitted for rental or loaner ski boots in case the only boots available are slightly less than snug. Whereas some skiers prefer to wear a second pair of socks to minimize friction on the feet, others prefer a single layer. New skiers should be aware of both options and the advantages of each. If using the two-sock system, the sock near the skin should be a synthetic wicking layer that draws moisture away from the skin.

Participants should have extra layers of warmth and safety items such as sunblock in their personal packs.

Day Packs and Leader Packs

This topic has been covered in chapter 3, but some items specific to Nordic skiing are important to bring. During every GO Winter program, regardless of whether we are working out of a school, community center, or base camp with the intention to return, we require our participants to carry a day pack. People of all ages need to learn self-sufficiency and personal responsibility when engaging in activities in the outdoors. The following is a basic list of what each person should carry:

- Extra change of clothes to meet the seasonal demand
- Extra mittens and hat
- Extra socks
- Water bottle (filled with water to start)
- Sunglasses
- Lip balm
- Personal medications and personal first aid kit
- Snack, if required
- Trail map if skiing in a ski park

The leader pack should include the leader's personal items as well as items the leader should carry for the group. The location will also dictate the need for other pieces of gear. A leader pack for an outing at a ski park with groomed trails, a warming hut, and support services would understandably be different from one for a wilderness ski tour. For a ski park outing, the leader's pack needs to include the following:

- All the items listed for participants, plus extra clothing that can fit the largest person in the group
- Trail map
- Cell phone
- Group first aid kit, medical forms, at-a-glance forms, program paperwork

- Extra snacks
- Thermos filled with hot water, hot chocolate, and a selection of teas and soups (for the participant who ends up cold and needs a quick pick-me-up)
- Spare ski tip

For a wilderness ski tour, the leader pack includes everything a ski park trip requires, as well as the following:

- Mechanism to purify water
- Map, compass, GPS unit or satellite communication system
- Tarp, bothy bag (size to meet the group), rope, webbing
- Saw, equipment for making fire, small stove, pot
- Closed-cell foam pad (three-quarter size)
- Repair kit and tools

This may seem excessive, but for a leader responsible for the well-being of a group in a remote setting, these are essential pieces of equipment.

Spare ski tip.
©Kevin Redmond

Getting Started

Starting a group ski outing at an established facility with some form of shelter is preferred. If participants do not have their own ski gear, the logical meeting place for fitting boots, distributing skis, organizing the group, and preparing everyone for the outing is where the ski equipment is stored.

Once outside, you should consider leading introductory activities in an open area. When participants are familiar with the techniques of skiing, you can progress to skiing on an established trail system and then to establishing your own trails in a familiar area.

If meeting at a trailhead, the plan is a bit different. Ensure that you have received all paperwork (medical forms, permission forms, and forms with height, weight, and shoe size information). If not, teachers and after-school organizers can be great sources of inside knowledge of groups.

Prior to the group's arrival, have all pieces of equipment laid out (with names) and ready for pickup. Skis may be organized sequentially by length to accommodate the variety of weights, corresponding pole length, and individual boot sizes. Once participants have chosen their boots, move them to the fitting location. Have a supply of moleskin available for people whose boots are close but not an exact fit, to minimize the risk of abrasion and blisters.

After the initial activities in the open area, perform a final gear check with the group before heading to the trails. Be sure to train participants in basic trail etiquette, as follows:

- When there is no set track, a skier overtaking a slower skier should call out "Passing on your left" and pass the slower skier when the trail ahead is visible, wide, and clear.

- In venues with a set track, the approaching skier calls "Track," and the slower skier steps outside of the track to permit the faster skier to pass. After the faster skier passes, the slower skier steps back into the track.

- In trails with two-way traffic, the general rule is to stay to the right. Use extreme caution on hills and turns, especially turns at the bottoms of hills.

- On one-way trails, the general rule is to stay to the right.

- When ascending using the herringbone or side-step technique, stay clear of the classic track wherever possible.

- If you fall, move off the track as quickly as possible to avoid being hit by approaching skiers. If possible, fill any holes in the snow surface to make the track safe for the next skier.

- If walking is necessary, stay to one side and avoid walking on set tracks.

- When stopped (e.g., for waxing, drinking, chatting), do so in an area where you are easily visible to approaching skiers, and step outside the track.

- Be courteous and helpful to fellow skiers.

Before heading out on your group outing, leaders should do the following:

- Check the weather forecast, and bring along proper clothing and equipment.

- Keep in mind that sunlight can burn even on cold and cloudy days. Bring protection from the sun and wind for both skin and eyes.

- Know your route. Bring a trail map, if possible.

- Bring sufficient water to stay hydrated, and be on guard for signs of frostbite and hypothermia.

- Understand the trail difficulty symbols to ensure that you ski within your abilities (see figure 7.1).

Nordic Skiing Activities and Games

When choosing Nordic ski activities and games for your groups, consider cross-curricular connections, age appropriateness (most people like to play, but you need to be discerning—what activity is safe and will work best?), and modifications to meet the physical needs and interests of your participants as well as the environment.

In all Nordic ski activities, ensure a minimum of two body lengths between participants and objects to avoid hazards, especially ski tips and pole points. For many modified or hybrid activities, we recommend that no poles be used.

The most important aspect of skiing is balance. This concept should be emphasized at every opportunity. The opening activities in this chapter focus on balance; if your participants really like them, you can continue to use them as warm-ups or fun activities throughout the unit.

Easy

More difficult

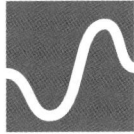

Most difficult

FIGURE 7.1   Trail difficulty symbols.

One-Ski Owl Hop

This is an introductory balancing activity adapted to skiing from a traditional summer, or fair-weather, activity used by indigenous people around the world.

Age or Grade Level

Any age or grade level

Number of Participants

Any number of participants; the activity is performed in pairs.

Equipment

Skis, no poles

Setup

Choose a relatively level area with plenty of space.

How to Lead

- The object of this activity is to outlast your opponent by continuously hopping on one foot.
- Participants stand on the ski foot of their choice and lift the other ski entirely off the snow.

- On cue, all participants begin to hop on their ski foot; the full ski must come off the snow on each hop.
- When one person loses balance, stops hopping, or allows the nonhopping ski to touch the snow, the contest is over. Both participants find new partners and begin again.
- Only one leg is used throughout a contest, but participants may use the other leg at the start of a new contest. Encourage them to alternate legs every contest to aid balance and develop strength in both legs.

Variations

- To make this a competitive event, the winner is the person who outlasts all other competitors.
- Use the snowy stork stance (which focuses on balance) as a lead-up (if participants are warmed up) or follow-up (if owl hop is used as a warm-up).

Safety Considerations

- Participants should maintain a personal space of approximately two ski lengths.
- Tell participants: "If you're going to fall, fall like a ball."

Solo and Tandem Scooter Ride or Race

The scooter activity simulates the desired effect of the classic diagonal stride and glide. In the scooter, it is step and push with the nonski foot followed by a glide on the ski leg. The terminology used to explain the diagonal stride is "kick and glide."

Age or Grade Level

Any age or grade level

Number of Participants

Any number of participants; the activity is performed in pairs.

Equipment

One ski for each participant, no poles

Setup

- Find a groomed classic track that is relatively level and preferably away from high-traffic areas.
- This is a learning activity and is likely to damage the track significantly; hence it is ideally done on a track intended for this purpose. You may wish to set a series of parallel tracks by having participants ski behind you in a straight line for approximately 50 to 100 meters.
- Instruct participants to always keep the nonski foot outside the groomed track (e.g., if the ski is on the left foot, the ski is in the right groove of the classic track and the right foot is outside the groomed track).

How to Lead

- The object of this activity is to step and propel with the nonski foot and then glide on the ski.

- When momentum begins to slow, push off with the nonski foot again. Participants continue to the end of the designated track and return.

- When participants have sufficient mastery on the first leg (or have fatigued that leg), they change the ski to the other foot and repeat.

- Only one leg is used at a time throughout this activity.

Variations

- The tandem scooter activity is done in pairs. Each partner wears one ski, and they stand side by side with their ski legs in the track and their nonski legs outside. Partners hold hands or arms and step and glide together down the track.

- The tandem scooter variation may be used as a lead-up to the solo scooter if participants have difficulty with balance.

- The tandem scooter may be used as a race or cooperative fun activity after the solo scooter activity.

Safety Considerations

- Participants should maintain a personal space of approximately two ski lengths.

- In the tandem scooter, instruct participants that, if they're going to fall, to fall like a ball to the side of their nonski foot—away from the track!

Unladylike Skiing

In the late 1800s skiing was considered unladylike in Norway, and women were encouraged to take up skating instead. The first all-woman ski club was established when Norwegian girls began to practice skiing in secret.

Mitten Tag

This frozen tag game helps skiers improve their mobility and balance while having fun.

Age or Grade Level

Any age or grade level

Number of Participants

Any number of participants

Equipment

- Spare mittens (or cotton gloves) balled up or soft throwables
- Skis, no poles (the unused poles may be used to mark the boundaries, though)

Setup

Premark the boundary of a playing area (e.g., field), or have participants follow you to mark the boundary. The size of the playing area should match the size of the group (e.g., a group of 15 to 25 would use approximately a third or half of a soccer field). You will need enough space so that participants can run around without bumping into each other.

How to Lead

- Number participants (e.g., from 1 to 20).
- Begin the activity by giving numbers 1 through 4 a mitten ball or throwable each. These players are taggers first.
- The taggers chase the others, throwing their objects and trying to strike them below the neck (headshots are not permitted).
- When a person is tagged, the tagger calls out that person's name to identify them as frozen (e.g., "Kelly's frozen!"). This is important because layers of winter clothing can make it difficult to feel a tag.
- Emphasize the importance of honesty and trust in this activity. For self-governance to work, every participant must contribute to the enjoyment of others.
- Frozen players must stand still with their arms outstretched. They can be freed by a hand-to-hand touch from another player. (Your group may come up with an alternative method.)
- When you sense that the taggers' turn has been long enough (e.g., after one or two minutes), stop the activity and designate another set of players (e.g., numbers 5 through 8) to be taggers.
- The activity may continue until everyone has been a tagger, or may conclude after a couple of introductory rounds.

Variations

Participants may play on one or two skis. Participants may play on one ski after learning the scooter activity. Later in the unit, after you have introduced the stride and glide on two skis with no poles, participants can play on two skis.

Safety Considerations

- All participants must stay at least one ski length from any other participant's skis to minimize the risk of being struck by a ski.
- If you use this activity at the beginning or in the middle of a session, modify the length and intensity so that participants are warm but not sweating. Sweat at the end of an activity session is acceptable if you are moving to an indoor venue or warming station.

Foxes and Hares Team Tag

The arctic fox and arctic hare, unique to northern areas, have extra layers of fur to survive the long, challenging winters. Like their southern counterparts, arctic foxes hunt arctic hares; in many areas the arctic hare is essential to the arctic fox's survival. Like mitten tag, this activity helps skiers improve their mobility and balance while having fun.

Age or Grade Level

Any age or grade level

Number of Participants

Any number of participants

Equipment

- One soft throwable per game
- Skis, no poles (the unused poles may be used to mark the boundaries)

Setup

Premark the boundary of a playing area (e.g., field), or have participants follow you to mark the boundary. The size of the playing area should match the size of the group (e.g., a group of 15 to 25 would use approximately a third or half of a soccer field). You will need enough space so that participants can run around without bumping into each other.

- If you have a large group, break the group into multiple games (e.g., two on two or three on three).

How to Lead

- The activity begins with a rock-paper-scissors to decide which team is "it" (foxes) to start. (Players wearing mittens should use an outstretched thumb perpendicular to fingers as scissors, and a tucked-in thumb parallel to fingers as paper.)
- All participants are free to go anywhere within the boundaries.
- Foxes work together to try to strike a hare with the object. They pass the object around to corner a hare or limit the hares' space and options.
- Hares who go outside the marked area are considered caught.
- Once a hare is caught, roles are reversed for the next round—the hares become foxes, and the foxes become hares.

Variations

Modify this game to suit the skill set of your participants and where you are in your unit. Participants may play on one or two skis. On one ski, they use the scooter technique; on two skis, the stride and glide or skate technique.

Safety Considerations

- All participants must stay at least one ski length from any other participant's skis to minimize the risk of being struck by a ski.
- If you use this activity at the beginning or in the middle of a session, modify the length and intensity so that participants are warm but not sweating. Sweat at the end of an activity session is acceptable if you are moving to an indoor venue or warming station.

Friskit

This hybrid game combines cricket and Ultimate but on skis.

Age or Grade Level

Age 10 and up

Number of Participants

Any number of participants; games of three on three or four on four are best.

Equipment

- One soft sponge disc per game
- Three or four ski poles to use as wickets
- Rope, ski poles, or Kool-Aid for marking the boundaries

Setup

- Premark the perimeter of the game area, or have participants follow you to mark the boundary.
- Before the game, each team prepares its own wickets using two or three ski poles as the wicket stumps (4 in., or 10 cm, between poles).
- You may use a bale through the pole straps, but they are not necessary and increase the setup time.
- Mark in (or with) snow a 6-foot (2 m) no-entry crease around the wickets (you can use one adult ski or two children's skis to measure).

How to Lead

- The rules of Ultimate apply, except there is no fighting for the disc to avoid person–ski collisions.

- Players have only three seconds (modify this time to five seconds if necessary) to pass the disc.
- When the disc is not caught, possession goes to the nearest opponent.
- The disc must hit one or more of the stumps to score.
- When a point is scored, the point-scoring team throws the disc to the other team to restart the game.

Variations

- Use a soft throwable in place of a disc.
- This may be played using any or all ski progressions, such as one-ski scooter, two-ski diagonal stride, or V skate.

Safety Considerations

- All participants must stay at least one ski length from any other participant's skis to minimize the risk of being struck by a ski.
- If you use this activity at the beginning or in the middle of a session, modify the length and intensity so that participants are warm but not sweating. Sweat at the end of an activity session is acceptable if you are moving to an indoor venue or warming station.

Hill Olympics: Skills for Hills

To climb hills, classic skiers use the side-step or herringbone technique; skate skiers use the offset, two-step, or one-step technique. Classic and skate ski descending techniques include the toe-knee-nose glide position, double pole, snowplow, snowplow pizza turn, and step turn. (See *Quality Lesson Plans for Outdoor Education* for more on these techniques.) Depending on the participants' skill level and your emphasis, any combination of these skills may be used in this activity.

Age or Grade Level

Any age or grade level

Number of Participants

Any number of participants

Equipment

- Skis
- Ski poles or spray bottle with colored water (food coloring or Jell-O) to mark boundaries
- Other equipment based on chosen obstacles

Setup

- This activity can be done with one large group or numerous smaller groups (two to five people).

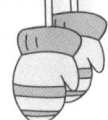

Types of Skiing Snow

Skiers in the early 1900s created terminology to describe various types of snow. Such terms included "pow pow," "mashed potatoes," "cauliflower snow," "sticky snow," and "dust on the crust." Mashed potatoes is an old, dense, heavy snow that is difficult to ski in!

- Participants design a slalom, circuit, or obstacle course for everyone to follow. This may be set up as a competition (timed or skill) or as a challenge obstacle course.

- The course should include only skills for hills already introduced.

- Ski poles or Kool-Aid can be used to mark areas or routes in the course.

- Each group is assigned its own hill.

How to Lead

- For beginning learners, place the emphasis on technique rather than speed. As skill levels advance, make this a timed event or add an emphasis on completing the activity more quickly.

- Challenge suggestions: 10-meter side-step ascent, 20-meter herringbone ascent, 100-meter diagonal stride, 20-meter double pole descent, 20-meter tuck glide, step turn out of the track, double pole, pizza or snowplow turn, double pole or tuck glide to the bottom of the hill, free skate or ski to the starting point, removing one ski, scooter to TV staging area and pose for the camera with the removed ski vertical and a nameplate near the face (optional interview to follow)

Variations

This may be run like a Tough Mudder race challenge or as a speed (timed) event.

Safety Consideration

When using ski poles to mark the course, ensure that they are secure in the snow throughout the event. If a pole becomes dislodged, pause the event if a skier is approaching the dislodged pole. Avoid conditions in which a skier may fall on a ski tip.

Sly Snail Mail

Age or Grade Level

Any age or grade level

Number of Participants

Any number of participants

Equipment

One small envelope or fist-size object (ball, soft toy)

Setup

This game is best played after instruction is completed and when participants are free to ski among the local trails.

How to Lead

- The mailbag (envelope or object) begins in your hands or in the hands of someone you designate.
- The object of the game is to secretly place the mailbag in the pocket or pack of an unsuspecting participant. If caught, the person with the mailbag must move on to someone else.
- A person who passes the mailbag without being caught waits a short time (10 seconds to 2 minutes) before quietly letting the person know or signaling that he or she has the mailbag.
- The person who now has the mailbag must deliver it to someone else.
- The game ends at the end of the lesson or activity time.

Variations

- Begin with an empty plastic baggie, and have every person add a small item (e.g., candy, coin—not snow or ice). The object is to not have the mailbag at the end of the game.
- Begin with the mailbag (sandwich bag containing allergy-free snack to be shared) in your hands. Offer a genuine compliment to a participant and pass on the mailbag. That person is free to sample (eat a small portion of) the mail before complimenting another skier and passing the mailbag to that person. No one may carry the mailbag twice; those offered the mailbag after already having it should decline. Compliments and passing the mailbag may be public or private. In a private version, a person who catches somebody passing the mailbag gets to take the mailbag, even if the person has already had a turn. Everyone in the group should receive at least one genuine compliment and the choice of a treat from the mailbag. The mailbag should finish with you so that you are the last to get a compliment and treat.

Safety Considerations

Do not have participants play this game during important instructions that require their undivided attention.

Relay Race, Obstacle Course, or Time Trials

This activity provides an opportunity to apply learned skills in a fun group setting.

Age or Grade Level

Any age or grade level

Number of Participants

Any number of participants

Equipment

Marking equipment such as snow cones, skis, or poles

Setup

- Setting the course up as a loop (starting and finishing at the same place) is ideal.
- Premark the activity boundary (start and finish), or have the group follow you as you mark it.
- The area should match the size of the group, and provide one lane for each group.

How to Lead

- Divide the group into teams of three to six. These directions assume teams of four.
- The first skier skis one lap using the classic ski technique.
- The second skier skis half a lap with classic ski and half a lap with kick-double pole.
- The third skier skis half a lap with classic and half a lap double pole.
- The fourth skier skis one lap using the skate skiing technique.

Variations

- You can include more basic or advanced skills depending on the terrain or participants' age or skill level.
- Basic skills may include stork stance for 20 seconds (five seconds added if balance is lost and the lifted foot touches snow), solo scooter, tandem scooter, and stride and glide with no poles.
- More advanced skills may include herringbone ascending, stride counting over a specific distance (the fewer strides, the better), and downhill step turns.
- You or the group may invent your own challenges.
- With participants in the same groups, have them perform the same skills on the same course at the end of each day as a time trial and record their times. As their skills improve, their times should decrease. Applaud personal and group bests.

Safety Considerations

- Technique is often sacrificed when racing. Encourage participants to maintain good technique to avoid injuring themselves or damaging ski equipment.
- When racing in close quarters, skiers need to keep the sharp tips of poles under control; trailing skiers also need to be aware of the poles of skiers ahead of them.

Ski Tour

The ski tour is ideally suited as a culminating activity at the end of the skiing unit. The route is off trail or longer than usual, and participants stay together.

Age or Grade Level

Any age or grade level

Number of Participants

Any number of participants

Equipment

- Flagging tape
- The leader pack, including a map and navigational aids
- Personal packs for the participants

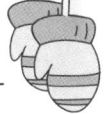

> ### *Ski Fitness*
>
> Cross-country skiing burns more calories per hour than any other sport! Depending on weight and speed, one can burn up to 1,200 calories per hour. It's easy to learn, low risk, and low impact.

Setup

You should be familiar with the route and current conditions. Consider using flagging tape to mark the route.

How to Lead

- Choose a lead skier and a trail (or sweep) skier.
- All participants must stay between the lead and sweep skiers.
- The lead skier stops at times for, among other things, safety, points of interest, navigational clarity, clothing management, hot spot or blister monitoring, water in/water out, pace control, and group management.
- Every skier should be assigned (or choose) a buddy.
- At regular intervals initiate a buddy-up, in which participants find their buddies. Then do a roll call. You might assign each buddy pair a number and have them call out their numbers in sequence: 1, 2, 3, 4, 5, 6 . . . .

Variation

Consider dividing large groups into smaller groups (e.g., a maximum of eight), each of which must stay close together. The entire group may meet at times throughout the tour.

Safety Considerations

- Avoid hazards such as avalanche areas, deep gulches, ravines, concealed water, and tree wells.
- Some form of communication (e.g., walkie-talkie) is recommended between the lead and sweep skiers so the sweep can inform the lead of any issues in the back of the group.

- The lead skier should be conscious of keeping the group together and establish a pace that fits the group.
- Know emergency exits in advance, and have protocols in place in the event that an emergency exit is required.

Extended Ski or Multiple-Activity Course

This activity is another potential peak experience that may include just Nordic ski skills or a variety of activities such as Nordic skiing, snowshoeing, winter trekking, and pulk or toboggan activities. The directions are general so that you can create your own course to fit your group and situation. The focus of this activity should be on challenge, camaraderie, and completion. The length and design should suit the age, fitness level, and skills of your participants.

Age or Grade Level

Any age or grade level

Number of Participants

Any number of participants

Equipment

- Markers or flagging to mark shorter routes.
- For extended distances, a map may be useful. Rather than having marked maps specially copied, you can mark the route on one map and have participants copy the route on a generic map, as is done in orienteering meets.
- Depending on your variation, ski, snowshoe, or pulk or toboggan gear may be required.

Setup

- This course can be anywhere from 1 to 20 kilometers (0.6 to 12 mi). Keep it on the shorter side if this is a first-time experience for your group.
- For shorter courses, marking or flagging should suffice. For extended routes, maps may be required.
- You can design your course using the natural terrain (e.g., hills as obstacles), or you can have participants design and build obstacles into the course (that you approve).
- At the finish line, consider having a warming hut and a treat (e.g., hot chocolate).

How to Lead

- This activity can be done on an individual basis, but we suggest that you make it a team event.

- Following are two possible approaches: (1) If it is a single activity (e.g., a ski-only event), record the time it takes for all team members to complete the course. (2) If it is a multiple activity (e.g., a ski and snowshoe event), have all members of each team stay together throughout the course with the object being to complete the course.
- Each team should have a leader who is responsible for making sure that all team members follow instructions.
- You can have a mass start or, if trail space is limited, a staggered start (e.g., groups leave one minute apart for short courses, two or three minutes apart for longer courses).

Variations

- Have a group of five that includes two skiers and two snowshoers (one pulling a pulk and the other alongside); the fifth person is the navigator and is in the pulk.
- This activity can be combined with navigation (map, compass, GPS), geocache, or treasure hunt challenges.

Safety Considerations

- Be very clear about the route to ensure that participants do not get lost.
- For longer courses, participants should carry extra food (e.g., energy bars) and water.

Reference

Redmond, K., Foran, A., & Dwyer, S. (2010). *Quality lesson plans for outdoor education*. Champaign, IL: Human Kinetics.

Extending the Experience: Camping and Trekking

Part IV

Chapter 8
Winter Camping

Many people fear winter camping because they are afraid they will be cold and miserable throughout the trip. We have found that with proper practice and progressive skill building, most people can enjoy a winter camping experience as much or more than they do a summer one. The joys of camping in winter include the lack of bugs and the fact that you often have the place to yourselves.

If your participants have developed the skills for being comfortable and happy outdoors on a day trip in winter, it's time to start planning and preparing for their first winter camping trip. An overnight winter trip requires an in-depth plan for dressing, eating, and sleeping. For a first outing, consider using a site that has an indoor or warm backup space. This way, anyone who gets really cold has a place to warm up for a bit.

Following is a checklist for preparing for winter camping:

- File a trip plan so people know when to expect you out of the field.
- Research the area that you will be traveling in, and be sure to have both an electronic and a paper copy of the map(s).
- Check road, parking, and trail conditions before departure.
- Pack extra food and clothing in case you get caught out longer than intended as a result of weather or trail conditions.
- Check the weather forecast frequently before departing, because storms can advance quickly in winter.
- Check the avalanche forecast before departing. Cancel the trip if the avalanche danger is high.

Staying Warm and Dry

The simple key to successful winter camping is staying warm and dry. When camping out in winter, we pack all of the gear we take for summer trips plus a few extra layers (discussed later). Staying warm and dry is an active process that continues throughout the time you are outdoors. As discussed in chapter 3, it's important to perfect your winter layering system so that you don't sweat. As physical activity levels go up (e.g., when snowshoeing or skiing), it's critical that you remind your participants to remove clothing layers until they are still warm but not hot, especially if you are spending the night outside. Sweating makes base layers damp; when physical activity stops, that dampness quickly brings a chill. Winter outings are a constant process of layers off, layers on, layers off, layers on. This is known as *venting*, whereby heat is shed and sweating prevented through the active process of adding and removing layers.

Creative Camping

When winter camping, it is important to remember that many things have multiple functions. For example, you can use your boots to keep your water from freezing, or use the leftover pasta water you melted as drinking water!

For winter camping, we like to pack what we call a big, fluffy layer. Depending on your climate, this insulating layer (most often a parka with a hood) can be made of down or synthetic fiber. This layer is ideally big enough to fit over all your other clothing. To capture and retain warmth, we have our participants put on their big, fluffy layers whenever we have slowed or stopped, such as during breaks and while cooking.

Hands and feet, both areas of the body with minimal built-in insulation, require special attention while winter camping. They are often the first body parts to be reported as cold and can lead to a miserable time if not kept warm. The secret to warm hands and feet is keeping them dry and having one's core temperature and metabolism well stoked. This is accomplished by eating well and choosing the right thickness of insulation, venting, eliminating constriction, and bringing spare clothing to change into if dampness reigns by the end of the day.

When winter camping, we bring two extra pairs of wool socks—one to put on in the early evening and one to wear while sleeping. Especially on longer trips, good foot health requires that our feet spend at least part of the day in a warm, dry place—thus, sleeping socks. I store my sleeping socks with my sleeping bag so they are always warm and clean and keep my feet happy during the night. If you're planning on digging a quinzhee or other snow shelter, it is critical that everyone have an extra pair of dry gloves or mittens to use in the evening. You might be tempted to add three or four layers to hands and feet in hopes of staying warm, but don't! This will constrict blood flow and actually make your hands or feet colder.

Making the shift from a day trip to winter camping may also require a change in boot selection. Boots that are ideal for winter camping have removable liners that can be dried overnight in sleeping bags or near a stove or fire. Those without removable liners can incorporate a vapor barrier liner (professionally made or a bread bag version) into the sock layer system to help keep the boot insulation material dry.

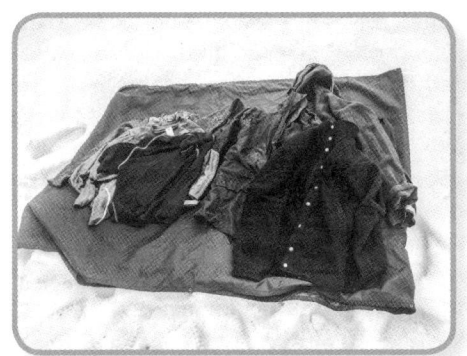 

Here's a sample of the types of clothing (a) and accessories (b) you'll want to pack in order to stay warm and dry while winter camping!
© Andrew Foran

We also bring sit-upons (small foam mats) to insulate our backsides from the cold while sitting or to stand on while cooking to keep our feet warm. After a very active day (e.g., skiing), everyone should have an extra set of base layers to change into.

Given the extra layers you need to be warm and dry while winter camping, you will likely need a bigger backpack than in summer. For an overnight trip, plan on a 60- to 80-liter (3,661-4,881 cu in.) backpack; for a longer trip, 80 to 120 liters (4,881 -7,323 cu in.), depending on whether you are using a sled to pull some of your gear. Packs with lash points are helpful in case you need to carry skis or snowshoes.

Eating, Drinking, and Cooking

Cooking and eating while winter camping need not be a chore. With shovels and some effort, you and your group can craft a kitchen any chef would be proud of. Start by piling snow and packing it down. Using a combination of shovel and snow saw, you can carve counters, tabletops, and seats for everyone in the group. You can also construct a windbreak for your stove, and a spice rack is a handy addition. The beauty of a snow kitchen is that if you happen to spill on a countertop, you can just pack fresh snow on top of it and the mess is gone!

Liquid-fuel stoves (rather than canister stoves) are recommended for use in cold temperatures. Before leaving, make sure your stove is working properly. A windscreen and heat exchanger improve winter cooking performance and reduce the amount of fuel required. You will use more fuel at higher elevations, and it takes extra fuel to melt snow into water. Plan on half to three-quarters of a liter (or quart) of fuel per stove per day depending on how efficient your group is with cooking. Finally, consider bringing a backup stove. Having two stoves can also speed up the snow-melting process and other cooking tasks. In extreme temperatures, stove fuel can be difficult to light. Keep your fuel in your shelter for the night, or warm it under your parka before use. When priming a white gas stove, you can prewarm the spirit cup with a lighter or match. Be prepared for having to hold a match or lighter to the fuel for a longer time than in summer to get it to ignite.

Don't Get Hungry!

While camping in the winter it is recommended that you pack at least 2 to 2.5 pounds of dry food with you for each day. Remember, your body needs lots of calories to generate heat!

On your first few winter excursions, keep the cooking fairly simple. Macaroni and cheese is a fine winter staple because it provides a combination of both carbohydrate and fat and is easy to cook. When planning meals for winter camping, keep in mind that the macronutrients (fat, protein, and carbohydrate) are how we stoke the fires of our metabolism. Having a well-stoked body is critical for staying warm. Simple sugars are like tinder. They are digested easily and quickly and provide a quick source of energy. Complex carbohydrates are like kindling. They burn a little slower but still provide an easy source of energy. Fat and protein are like the fuel logs we put on a fire overnight; they burn slow and long. Most meals have a combination of all three macronutrients, but fat and protein are especially important at suppertime.

One of the joys of winter camping is that you get to eat a lot more than when camping the rest of the year. In general, for winter camping you should plan on 3,500 to 5,000 calories per person per day. Simple sugars, complex carbohydrates, and protein all contain 5 calories per gram. Fat contains 9 calories per gram, which makes it an efficient source of fuel for winter camping. Often in winter, we split the larger group into smaller cooking groups that plan their menus together and then prepare their own food in the field. This gives everyone more ownership over the menu and more practice cooking and using the stoves.

Because most of your food will freeze in the winter, a few preparatory tasks can help. Precut all of your cheese and meat into small squares before going into the field. The small squares are easily melted in mouths during lunch stops and warm up quickly for dinners. Consider removing wrappers from candy and granola bars, because they can be very tricky to unwrap in the wind with big mittens on. Unwrapping and bulk bagging food before you go is an easier way to deal with litter in the winter. Pretest some of the food you are considering taking on a winter camping trip by placing it in the freezer and then trying to eat it. You don't want to break your teeth on a frozen chocolate bar or a stick of salami.

Staying well hydrated when winter camping keeps everyone happy and healthy. Well-hydrated people are also less likely to get either frostbite or hypothermia. Cold water in the winter, however, is less appetizing than warm, so it's important to stop the group frequently to drink out of thermoses, or to stop and have a boil-up. Many people use insulated mugs during winter camping to keep their hot drink hot. I prefer a half-liter Nalgene bottle rather than an insulated mug because it warms me in two ways: I can hold the bottle to warm my hands, or place it in my parka to warm my core. In my jacket, the hot drink stays hot, and I can sip on it at will.

When headed out on a day trip, you can likely carry all the water you will need. When winter camping, however, you will likely need to melt snow. Always have a little water to start the process of melting snow to keep the pot from scorching the snow. Burnt snow is yucky! Start with about a cup of water in the bottom of the pot and slowly add snow. Do not add too much snow too quickly. As water accumulates in the pot, you can add more snow. Because melting snow is a fuel-intensive process, determine whether you're just melting snow or whether you are preparing hot drinks. If you are preparing hot drinks, once there's enough water in the pot, stop adding snow and allow the water to come to a boil. "Making water" is a common evening camp chore. Sending everyone to bed with at least 2 liters (or quarts) of water makes it possible to have hot drinks with breakfast without having to spend a lot of time melting snow.

Once snow is melted into water, you don't want it to freeze again. This is accomplished in one of several ways. You can build a snow fridge—a rectangular cutout in your snow kitchen. Place your pot of water or water bottles in the opening and then place a snow block door to seal off the water from the environment. If you place your water bottles upside down, the threads are less likely to freeze shut. Wide-mouthed water bottles are preferable for winter camping because their lids take longer to freeze shut than smaller ones do. You can also keep your water bottles in your sleeping shelter, tucked under or between sleeping bags.

If it is really cold out, you will all need to keep your water bottles inside your sleeping bags. To sleep warm, consider taking hot water bottles to bed. They prewarm the sleeping space and provide a ready source of hydration in the night. The seal of these water bottles must be trustworthy to avoid getting wet from spilled water. Testing water bottle lid seals several times is a must before placing them in sleeping bags.

The sun sets early in the winter, making the nights long. Make sure your headlamp and flashlight batteries are new or fully charged before the trip, and always take extras. Lithium batteries are often chosen for winter excursions because they perform well in cold weather. Cold temperatures are hard on all batteries, decreasing how long they are usable. For maximal performance, try to keep batteries warm by keeping them in pockets next to your body. Sleep with your battery-operated devices and extra batteries inside your sleeping bag to keep them warm.

Building a Shelter

The many options for winter camping shelters range from snow shelters to four-season mountaineering tents to traditional wall tents. They require different amounts of setup time and provide varying degrees of comfort. It is important to choose accommodations that fit with your participants' skill level and needs, and your resources.

Snow Shelters

Digging a shelter out of snow is a lot of work but results in a relatively warm and quiet place to spend the night. A snow trench is the easiest and fastest shelter to build; two to three hours may be needed to complete a snow cave, quinzhee, or igloo. To build a snow shelter, you need a snow shovel and, for igloos, a snow saw. Before digging, use a probe to make sure you won't be digging into a rock or buried tree. For beginner participants, we often bring a tent as a backup shelter.

Snow Trench A snow trench is typically used as a temporary bivouac or an emergency shelter for one or two people because it is relatively quick and easy to construct. It will not be as comfortable or warm as the other snow shelters. As a safety concern, during heavy snowfalls, do not use a snow trench because the weight of additional snow could easily collapse the roof. Here are directions for construction:

What Kind of Shelter?

If you need an emergency shelter, build a snow trench; it's the quickest to make. Quinzhees are ideal for soft snow without a slope. Igloos are a good option when you have several feet of solid, hard-packed snow. Whichever type of shelter you build, be sure that the door is lower than the floor so that the heat is trapped inside.

1. For one person, dig a trench in the snow at least 3 feet (1 m) deep, 3 to 5 feet (1 to 1.5 m) wide, and about 6 feet (2 m) long.
2. Dig a sloping entrance at the foot end.
3. Bridge the width of the trench with skis, poles, or tree branches.
4. Place a tarp, tent fly, or emergency blanket over the roof supports, and anchor the sides with snow. Tuck in and secure the foot end with additional snow.
5. Enter and exit the shelter carefully to avoid dumping snow on your sleeping system.

Snow Cave   Snow caves can be dug in areas with lots of snow. They are frequently dug into snow that has drifted into high banks. Two important safety rules are not digging a snow cave in an area that is at risk for an avalanche, and ensuring that your snow cave has adequate ventilation. For your first snow cave, start small; as you become more skilled, you can make larger ones. Snow caves are impressively strong, but must be dug out in the shape of a dome so the roof is adequately supported. Here are the construction directions:

1. Start digging at the base of the snowdrift. Always keep one person outside with a shovel in case the snow cave collapses. This person can quickly dig out the diggers.
2. Dig a tunnel into the drift. This tunnel should ideally slope upward so that colder air will sink down and out of the shelter.
3. Once the tunnel is 2 or 3 feet (0.5 to 1 m) long, begin to hollow it out into a dome. Send snow out of the tunnel on a sled if you have one. Avoid making the cave too wide, and have a plan for what to do if the roof collapses.
4. Make the inner dome large enough to fit your needs, but keep the roof 2 to 3 feet (0.5 to 1 m) thick. Before removing all of the snow, make some snow benches to sleep on. Colder air sinks below the bench, so you will sleep warmer.
5. Once you have hollowed out the interior, smooth the roof until there are no hard edges or shovel lines so you don't get drips on your sleeping bags.
6. It is critical to make a ventilation hole in the roof of your snow cave to avoid the risk of suffocation. Use a ski pole basket to punch a 4-inch (10 cm) hole in the roof.
7. Use a waterproof tarp to cover the floor to keep snow off your sleeping gear.
8. You can use a backpack or a sled in the doorway to keep the snow cave warmer; just make sure the door can still be opened if snow falls during the night.

Quinzhee   A quinzhee can be built in areas where the snow is not deep enough for a snow cave and not firm enough for an igloo. Our participants have built quinzhees with as little as 4 inches (10 cm) of snow on the ground. Two important safety rules are not digging a quinzhee in an area that is at risk for an avalanche, and ensuring that your quinzhee has adequate ventilation. For your first quinzhee, start small; as you become more skilled, you can make larger ones. Quinzhees are impressively strong, but must be dug out in the shape of a dome so that the roof is adequately supported. Quinzhees can be built for one to four people. Here are the construction directions:

1. Stomp out a circle in the snow. This circle should be large enough to have all group members lie down within it with a buffer at the head and feet; for a group of 5 to 10 builders, this would be a 8- to 10-foot (2.4 to 3 m) diameter.

2. Start piling snow in the circle. To save some time piling snow, you can bury nonessential gear in the middle of the pile. This means less snow to pile up and less snow to dig out. Just be sure not to bury your stove, pots, or extra layers.

3. As you pile the snow, whack it with the shovel to start the process of sintering (i.e., snow crystal bonding). Make sure the pile is rounded like a dome rather than pointy like a pyramid.

4. Once you have a pile that is 6 to 7 feet (1.8 to 2.1 m) high, pack and smooth the surface of the dome. Place small sticks or pieces of spaghetti into the pile at regular intervals to a depth of 8 inches (20 cm). This will help you ensure the proper wall and roof thickness during the digging-out process.

5. Let the snow pile sinter for one to two hours. This is a good time to enjoy a hot drink or meal or do an activity with your group.

6. Start digging at the base of the pile. Always keep one person outside with a shovel in case the quinzhee collapses. This person can quickly dig out the diggers.

Before removing all of the snow, make some snow benches to sleep on.

1. Dig a tunnel into the pile. This tunnel should slope upward so that colder air will sink down and out of the shelter. You can dig the tunnel from two directions to speed up the process.

2. Once the tunnel is 2 to 3 feet (0.5 to 1 m) long, or the two ends are connected, begin to hollow out the tunnel into a dome. Send snow out of the tunnel on a sled if you have one.

3. Make the inner dome large enough to fit your needs, but be careful to keep enough thickness in the walls and roof (8 in., or 20 cm). When you see the end of a stick or piece of spaghetti, stop digging at that spot. Before removing all of the snow, make some snow benches to sleep on. Colder air sinks below the bench, so you will sleep warmer.

4. Once you have hollowed out the interior, smooth the roof until there are no hard edges or shovel lines so you don't get drips on your sleeping bags.

5. It is critical that you make a ventilation hole in the roof of your quinzhee to avoid the risk of suffocation. Use a ski pole basket to punch a 4-inch (10 cm) hole in the roof.

6. Use a waterproof tarp to cover the floor to keep snow off your sleeping gear.

7. You can use a backpack or a sled in the doorway to keep the quinzhee warmer; just make sure the door can still be opened if snow falls during the night.

Igloo   An igloo can be built when snow conditions permit the cutting of snow blocks. Sometimes these conditions occur naturally, and sometimes people work-harden a snow quarry with skis or snowshoes to enable them to cut blocks. Two important safety rules are not building an igloo in an area at risk for an avalanche, and ensuring that your igloo has adequate ventilation. For your first igloo, start small; as you become more skilled, you can make larger ones. Igloos are impressively strong, but must be constructed in the shape of a dome so the roof is adequately supported. Here are the construction directions:

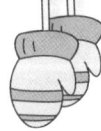

Toasty As an Igloo

Did you know that an igloo can be a hundred degrees warmer inside than outside? Because the compacted snow used to make igloos consists mostly of trapped air, it can't transfer heat and therefore insulates very effectively.

1. Level a space in the snow for your igloo.

2. Cut snow blocks from a snowdrift or your snow quarry using a shovel or snow saw. Keep the blocks the same size. The first set of snow blocks should be thicker than those used in subsequent rows. Cut the first few blocks on a diagonal.

3. Form the first row of blocks into a circle.

4. Make a second tier on top of the first by decreasing the block thickness and staggering the block joints.

5. Keep cutting and stacking blocks. As you build upward, gradually decrease the block thickness so that the upper rows are thinner and tapered toward the center of the igloo to form a dome.

6. It is critical that you make a ventilation hole in the roof of your igloo to avoid the risk of suffocation. Use a ski pole basket to punch a 4-inch (10 cm) hole in one of the blocks, or leave a gap between two of the blocks that form the roof.

7. Fill any gaps between blocks with snow.

8. Dig an entrance tunnel into your igloo, ideally at a sloping angle.

9. Smooth the blocks on the inside of the igloo to minimize dripping water.

10. Make some snow benches to sleep on.

Nylon Tents

If sleeping in a snowball (i.e., snow shelter) seems too much for a first outing, a nylon tent is quicker and easier to set up in winter conditions. A four-season nylon tent is better than a three-season tent because it is stronger and better able to handle the wind and snow loads of winter. For mild to moderate winter conditions, a good three-season nylon tent will likely suffice. The difference between a three-season and four-season nylon tent comes down to shape, pole strength, vestibule size, and guy line attachment points (four-season tents have extras). Four-season tents are usually heavier and more expensive than three-season tents. Here are a few hints for setting up and using a nylon tent in winter:

1. Pack down a level platform of snow using skis or snowshoes before setting up your tent.
2. Set up your tent beside this platform, and then move it onto the platform. This avoids having deep footprints in your sleeping area.
3. Dig out all or part of your vestibule to make it easier to put boots on.
4. Have a small brush handy to remove any snow that enters the tent.
5. Make sure to adequately ventilate your tent by opening the door zippers at the top. This allows water vapor from your breathing and clothes to escape. If you zip the door tight, you will wake up in the morning covered in frost.
6. Guy out your tent to protect it from blowing away in a high wind and to pull out the sides of the tent as much as possible.
7. In windy conditions, build a snow wall either directly beside the windward side of the tent or about 10 feet (3 m) away from the tent to break the wind and reduce drifting.

Sleeping Warm and Dry

No matter what type of shelter you choose to sleep in, there are some things you can do to ensure that you have a good night's sleep. When choosing a sleeping bag, make sure it's rated to at least 10 °C (18 °F) lower than the coldest temperature you expect to encounter. If you do not have a winter sleeping bag, you can put one summer sleeping bag inside another. Winter bags are insulated with either goose down or synthetic insulation. Down is often more expensive than synthetic materials, but it has a superior warmth-to-weight ratio. Down bags must remain dry because they lose their insulating capacity when wet (new weather-treated down sleeping bags are relatively expensive). Synthetic bags retain some ability to keep you warm when wet, but they are bulkier, heavier, and less compressible than down bags. Winter bags often have a hood to keep your head warm, a tube to keep drafts from coming through the zipper, and a draft collar above the shoulders. Using a sleeping bag liner can add extra warmth, minimize wear, and keep the sleeping bag cleaner. The extra layer can add 10 to 15 °C (18 to 27 °F) of warmth.

Potty Tips

When camping in the winter it is important to get up to use the bathroom in the night; if you don't, your body will be using extra energy to keep urine warm. That's energy that could be used to keep the rest of your body warm! It is also suggested that campers poop in an area with southern exposure, which allows for the best freezing and thawing and in turn kills all pathogens in the waste and disposes of it quickly.

Sleeping pads provide both cushioning and insulation from the snow. For winter camping, we recommend using two full-length pads to keep your body heat from being conducted to the cold ground. I like to use a combination of a thin closed-cell foam bivouac pad next to the ground and a self-inflating sleeping pad on top of it to get the best insulation from the snow and to have some redundancy in my sleeping system in case the self-inflating pad gets a puncture hole and can't be repaired. Sleeping pads are rated, like house insulation, in R-values, ranging from 1.0 to 8.0. The higher the R-value, the better protection it provides from the cold. You'll want a minimum R-value of 4.0 for winter comfort, and you can add the R-values of your two pads to achieve that result.

With your toasty sleeping bag and adequate insulation under you, here are a few more ways to bring more warmth to your night:

- Take your sleeping bag out of its stuff sack early in the evening so that it has a chance to decompress and reach its full loft.

- Use a hot water bottle or chemical heat pack to prewarm your sleeping bag. Be sure you trust the seal on your water bottle, and don't ever place chemical heat packs directly on skin.

- Go to bed warm. Do a few jumping jacks or take a short walk before getting into your sleeping bag. Think of an oven. Your sleeping bag is the insulation, and you are the heat coil. A cold body means a cold bag. You can also do sit-ups or push-ups in your bag to generate some heat.

- Go to bed dry. Change into dry base layers if the ones you have been wearing all day are damp. The same goes for your socks—replace damp socks for warm, dry, and clean sleeping socks.

- Wear a hat and neck gaiter to bed. They will keep these two areas of your body that lose heat quickly better insulated.

- Experiment with the amount of clothing you wear to bed. Some people are comfortable with solely base layers, whereas others need several layers. Try to find the right combination that keeps you warm enough but not so warm that you sweat.

- Have a high-calorie and fat-containing snack before bed to amp up your metabolism.

- Have a hot drink before bed, and be sure to pee before getting comfy in your sleeping bag. Consider having a pee bottle to use during the night so you don't have to go out in the cold. Female urine redirection devices make this process easy for women.

- On sunny mornings, put your sleeping bag out to dry before packing it away. Tie it to the top of your tent, or hang it from your ski tips. Be sure to tie it on so it doesn't blow away.

- On longer winter expeditions, consider using a vapor barrier liner in your sleeping bag to keep water vapor (i.e., your sweat) from entering the insulation.

Summary

Camping in winter is a magical experience. The crunch of snow underfoot, the dancing starlight, and the quiet woods combine to create an experience not soon forgotten. Once your participants are comfortable spending the day outside, you can consider trying your first winter camping trip. By following the suggestions in this chapter, you can have a fun, safe, and rewarding night out, whether you choose to sleep in a quinzhee, igloo, or nylon tent. The most important thing to remember is that sweat is evil; you must all manage your clothing systems to stay warm and dry. The second most important thing to remember is to eat and drink often to have plenty of energy to keep warm and attend to the camping tasks at hand. Most of all, look out for each other, stay active out there, and have fun.

Chapter 9

Winter Trekking: The Snow Expedition

When considering a winter expedition—a multiple-day and -night trip—you need to take a number of things into consideration. We raise just a few of the big topics in this chapter, as follows: planning, packing for, and dressing for extended winter trips; specialized equipment and skills; and essential camp skills (also see chapter 8, Winter Camping). By the time you are considering leading extended winter outings, you should have experienced numerous winter outings as well as camping trips, and feel confident in your ability to support others in winter environments.

Everything you need to address for any expedition (e.g., route, menu, emergency procedures, weather forecast, clothing) takes on a different element in winter. Cold (in some instances, deep cold) will be your greatest challenge as a GO leader. However, the rewards from hauling gear over snow-covered portage trails, woodland paths, and frozen lakes; pitching a winter tent; and preparing the evening meal on a portable woodstove are worth every snowy step!

Hauling Gear in Winter

This section addresses the advantages of sleds, toboggans, and pulks for hauling winter gear. Traditional toboggans, used by the Cree and Inuit people to transport supplies, were made of wood. They had no runners on the bottom, and the front was a curved hood—a J shape. Sleds typically had runners on the bottom, but over time, like toboggans, they evolved into recreational equipment. Runners, which are added weight and another source or repair when broken, are now a thing of the past on many sledding and toboggan hills.

Toboggans are made primarily from ash trees (the wood is strong and light), and they require regular maintenance to keep the bottom waxed and sliding freely. Modern toboggans are made of plastic and require very little maintenance. However, winter is winter, and if moisture comes into contact with the bottom of an icy-cold toboggan, frost will build up and we can promise you that you will be going

Snow Kitchen

When camping you can build a kitchen outside of your snow shelter by carving out things in the snow. This gives you places to cook as well as store food!

nowhere! Toboggans can get wet as a result of contacting lake slush (water trapped between the ice and snow layers that bubbles up through cracks), breaking through into a hidden pool when snowshoeing, crossing a brook or wet spot (a ground spring, or pooling due to melting or runoff), or simply just being outside on a cold night. On the trail, we pack a windshield scraper to scrape the bottoms of the toboggans to keep them sliding well.

Toboggans can haul a tremendous amount of gear. However, just because they are loaded does not mean they can be hauled! There is a breaking point that you must discover by trial and error—how much can you haul in snow, and what can your participants haul? How do hills affect your ability to keep moving? Toboggans work best on open pathways, and the flatter the surface is, the easier the hauling will be. If hauling with ropes, you will need a brake line at the back and disconnect yourself from the harness when going downhill.

Remember from chapter 3 that a pulk is a sled with a fixed rope or pole harness system to keep it from overtaking you on descents. Like toboggans, pulks have limits, which are magnified in deep, powdery snow and on inclines. One thing we can guarantee is that hauling your own freight toboggans or pulks offers a fantastic workout!

Pulks also need to be scraped down periodically. Using a wax product (e.g., MaxWax) can cut down on the need to scrape. Pulks are pulled via a harness system attached to two fixed rods that are attached to a sled. We have found that hip belts do the job, but they are not comfortable with heavy loads over long distances. An advantage of the pulk over the toboggan is that the sled tracks close behind the hauler, which is helpful in wooded terrain. Also, going downhill is easier than with toboggans because the fixed rods prevent the sled from chasing the hauler and smashing into the heels and legs (not a fun experience). Surprisingly, pulks can accommodate a lot of gear, and they are wonderful for solo or small trips or as supports for group trips. Outfitting an entire GO group with pulks may be challenging, but there is always the do-it-yourself (DIY) approach. We have a few DIY pulks in our fleet, and they are great.

a

b

Loaded and ready to haul into the North River Wilderness Area, Cape Breton, Nova Scotia (*a*); heading into the highlands, Antigonish, Nova Scotia (*b*).
© Andrew Foran

Toboggans make the most sense for us, given the location of our trips. We have found that the average person joining us on an overnight trip requires approximately 3.5 feet (1.1 m) of toboggan space for personal gear (we cover this in more detail later in this chapter). Don't forget the group gear you will also need to support a winter expedition. Figure 9.1 provides a starting point for planning a group trip. This is not an absolute schematic, but it can help with planning. It is based on 11-foot (3.4 m) and 7-foot (2.1 m) toboggans for a group of 12 with two leaders.

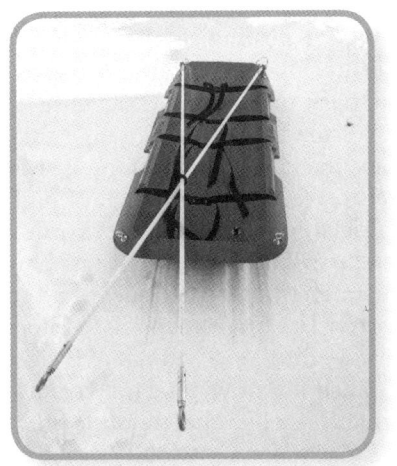
a

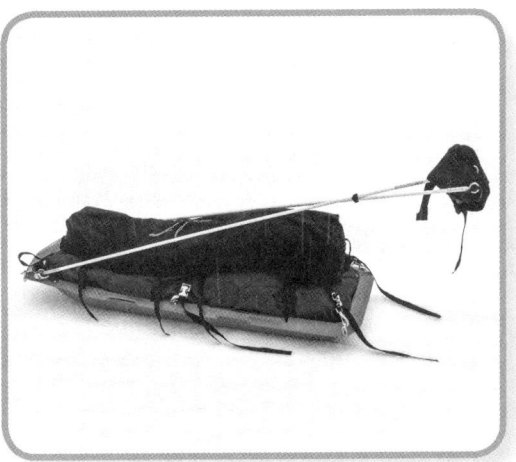
b

A homemade pulk (*a*) and a packed pulk (*b*).
© Andrew Foran

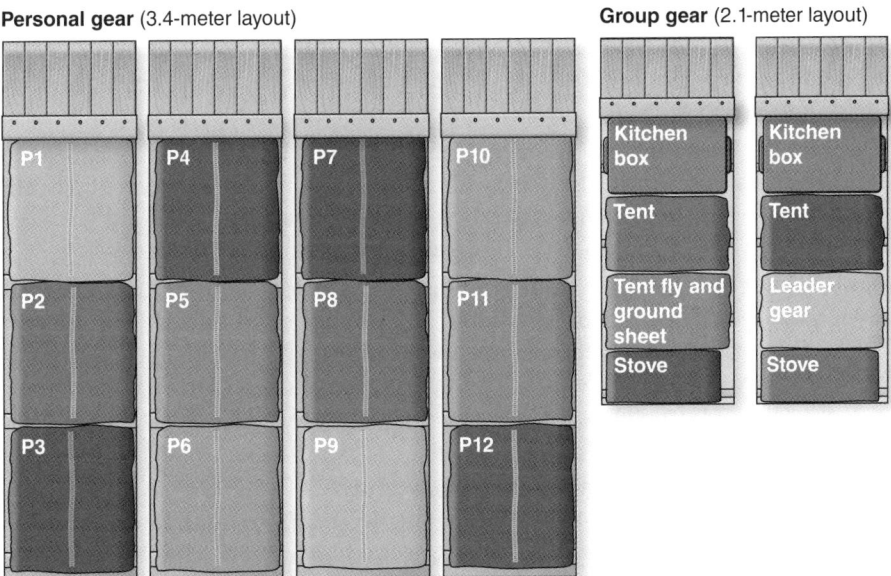

FIGURE 9.1 Layout for personal and group gear for a group of 12.

Group Gear

In addition to leader gear and participant gear, you will need to bring group gear—equipment you all need to travel and camp comfortably together in the winter. Following is our recommended list. You may discover items to add as you experiment with your own groups.

- **Stoves.** It is winter, and it will be cold. The wonderful thing about hauling gear with toboggans is that you can bring stoves. We were hoping you noticed that in figure 9.1 there's a woodstove for each tent. That means warmth! We highly recommend small portable woodstoves with folding legs, nesting stovepipe lengths (complete with a damper) and an elbow (to create an exit angle for the stovepipe), a warming shelf, a foil reflector, and a hearth (spark mat)—all packable inside the wood box for transport. We recommend stoves made of least 22 gauge steel. We always pack an extra adjustable elbow in case the elbow splits along a seam when adjusting (this does happen now and again). We also bring a roll of high-temperature aluminum foil tape in case a seam lets go during regular burning (this provides a quick fix until the new elbow can be installed). By the way, I have had an elbow separate because I forced an adjustment, but I have never had an elbow fail during a burn—but better safe than sorry. The final stove-related item, small but important, is a strand of wire about 6 feet (2 m) long with an oversized toggle attached to each end. The wire is used to attach the stove pipe to two sticks that cross to make a cradle (do not tie into a live tree—when the wind blows, so will your stove). The toggles give you something to grab on to without removing your mittens.

- **Bucksaws.** To use the woodstoves, you will need to cut dead standing hardwood for heat. We recommend a folding type of saw (exposed blades tend to tear gear in transit and while packing) or one with a reliable blade cover. Keep in mind that you will need to cut standing dead wood into stove lengths; I have a little piece of tape on my blades to indicate the length that will fit into my stove. We list a saw under group gear because wood gathering is a shared camp chore. Younger participants should do so only under leader supervision.

- **Clothesline.** Each tent should have a length of rope, with a bunch of carabiners to attach clothes to the line. This clothesline fixed to points at the peak of a heated tent provides the opportunity to dry sweat- or snow-soaked clothes and gear. And believe us—it will get very toasty at the peak of the tent.

- **Candle lanterns.** We encourage headlamps for personal use, but each group also needs to see as camp chores unfold in the evening and dark morning hours. These lanterns enclose the candles (**no open flame**), and surprisingly, a few lanterns in each tent can provide enough lumens to work by. We recommend beeswax candles; they burn clean with minimal wax waste, and they last longer than regular candles.

- **Kitchen boxes.** You may have noticed that figure 9.1 shows a space for a kitchen box, which can be plastic or wood. We use kitchen boxes to organize kitchen supplies and food for the trip (see the Cooking section later in this chapter for a list of kitchen supplies). If you decide to use plastic boxes, make sure they are resistant to cold. The manufacture specs will list the temperature they can withstand; if no temperature is listed, it's no good in the cold and will crack.

- **Tent.** We use expedition-size tents that are 10 by 15 feet (3 by 4.6 m) and can accommodate between six and eight people. The more people you have inside, the less personal equipment they can bring in with them (not an issue when you can wrap excess baggage with the McGee tarp, which is discussed later). These tents resemble the classic prospector tents, but they come with lightweight aluminum poles that are easy to assemble (no need to cut tree poles to make a frame). They are made from a lightweight 7-ounce (198 g) marine-grade cotton that is preshrunk (duck canvas) and treated to be water repellent, mildew resistant, and flame retardant. These tents breathe, allowing built-up moisture to escape, while shedding rain.

- **Groundsheets and flys.** We use groundsheets made from a cold-resistant 10-ounce (283 g) rubberized tarp. This is used in place of cutting spruce bows to make a tent floor. We also bring along a fly for each tent in case we are hit with a heavy, wet snow or rain (we have encountered heavy rains and freezing rain and not had one leak!). If you plan to leave a tent standing for long periods of time (e.g., as a base camp), use the fly to prevent snow buildup on the roof.

- **McGee tarps.** Each toboggan comes with a canvas or nylon tarp to wrap the base load (more on this later in the chapter). The McGee tarp, named after Sam McGee (from a classic winter poem to be read by the woodstove), serves to keep snow out of the wrapped gear. You could use what is called a tank: a canvas wrap with square ends that tie right to the running lines of the toboggan. I like the tank because the square, fixed ends keeps things from squirting out. Others I trek with like the tarps because they are another layer to cover the groundsheet or wrap up gear outside the tent. It's about preference.

- **Shovels.** We said this is winter, right? Shoveling snow is one camp chore that you will never be free of (this will keep you in shape for when you return to your driveway!). A good shovel for moving snow is essential. Based on the demands of setting up camp, consider bringing at least two shovels per tent.

- **Ice chisel.** Because your group will need lots of water for cooking, cleaning, and hydrating, accessing fresh water is essential. And what do we know about water in winter? That's right, it freezes. Choose a location where water is available, but remember that lakes, ponds, and streams may be frozen. You could melt snow on a woodstove, but this can be time-consuming. With an ice chisel you can make a hole in the ice at the edge of a lake or pond. Make sure it has a leash attached—in case it slips out of your hand and keeps going, only to be recovered in the spring!

- **Toboggans.** Toboggans should have running lines and straps to secure the base load, along with a tumpline (a line that goes around your waist or across your shoulders for hauling the load).

- **Conover packs.** Conover packs are long packs that attach to the toboggan's wrapped base load. Think of these as day packs for toboggans. Things to store in them include a thermos, a first aid kit, extra mittens and hats, a parka when hauling (you don't want to overheat), lunch, snacks, water, an ice scraper, a saw (for clearing windfalls along the trail), and any other equipment you might need while traveling. The point is to have gear you can access quickly without having to go into the base load that is securely wrapped to the toboggan. Conover packs are named after Garrett and Alexandra Conover, the authors of *Snow Walker's Companion: Winter Camping Skills for the North*.

- **Snowshoes.** These should be sized to fit each participant.

Leader Gear

Leader gear should accompany any trip to support all participants and ensure their safety. The following is a suggested list that you may want to add to:

Ice Thickness

Wondering if it's safe to traverse an icy pond? For a group to walk safely on ice, the ice should be at least 20 centimeters (about 8 inches) thick. The color of the ice can give you a hint about its depth. It is strongest when its appears clear blue; if it is white or snowy, it may only be half as strong as clear blue ice is. If the ice is gray, it is not safe to walk on.

- **Saw.** Carrying a few extra blades with your saw is prudent. Learning to cut dead standing wood takes practice, and it is especially challenging in deep snow. As participants learn this skill, blades can become block-pinched (snagged between two pieces of a log) and break.

- **Hatchet or forest ax.** A forest ax can help with felling (supporting the bucksaw), and a hatchet is perfect for splitting wood. We also recommend a file system to keep the blades sharp. Processing wood is a skill you will need to teach your participants, depending on their age. This group chore should always be done under leader supervision. Each log will need to be cut into blocks (sections that can fit into the woodbox of the stove), and each block split into segments. Many segments will then need to be cut into splits (kindling-sized pieces for starting and stoking the fire). The ability to make splits, and a lot of them, is the difference between a cold night in camp and a warm camp with cheery winter trekking mates! We bring a few small grocery bags of splits from home. This supply of seasoned wood gives our tent a head start in heating up, and the wood from the field has time to surface dry and warm up. During the evening, we make sure to refill the bags if we have additional nights ahead of us. These bags of splits can be stored in the McGee tarp or under the hood of the toboggan.

- **Fire making materials.** You will of course need matches and lighters for starting fires. Keep these warm, or they may fail in deep cold!

- **Map.** Carrying a map or maps is crucial, and so is knowing the area well and in all seasons. When planning your route, anticipate that progress can be hampered by the environment (this is winter, and you will be traveling by snow). Deep snow, cold, falling snow—these and more can slow your group down, so have camp backups.

- **Compass and GPS unit, along with a satellite communication system (e.g., SPOT).** You need to know where you are and where you are going. GPS and satellite systems provide a bit more assurance, but they should not replace a solid trip plan.

- **Cell phone.** Like GPS and satellite systems, a cell phone can help, but it should not replace a solid trip plan.

- **First aid kit.** The leaders' first aid kit not a personal participant ouch pouch; this is a properly stocked kit that can support everyone on the trip. Make sure your first aid kit is winterized, and check it before every outing. We tie off the zippers with an electrical tie to let us know whether the kit has been opened. If the tie is secure, it is good to go. If the tie is cut or missing, we know we need to do an inventory to see if anything is missing.

- **Backcountry stove.** While traveling, you may need to heat up food or boil water quickly. A one-burner stove is a great alternative to your woodstoves when you are on the go. Choose a stove that works exceptionally well in winter conditions.

- **Thermos.** Every leader should have a thermos filled with hot water. This supply is ready to use if needed on the trail (a hot drink for a participant in need) and while camp is under construction.

- **Rope bag.** I don't think we need to say much about the usefulness of rope when camping and traveling. In addition to rope, we bring three or four pieces of 1-inch (2.5 cm) webbing that's 8 to 10 feet (2.4 to 3 m) in length, which is as useful as rope and easier to hold on to with mittens and gloves.

- **Bothy bag.** For trips of any duration, we like to use a bothy bag for an immediate group shelter. A bothy is like a parachute that the group can pull over until everyone is inside; the largest size can accommodate up to 20 people. A bothy allows for a quick reprieve from the elements, a shelter in which to care for participants or make gear repairs—a bubble to give the group a break.

- **Repair kit.** Your repair kit should contain any tools and equipment you will need to repair your gear.

A group inside a bothy bag.
© Andrew Foran

- **Water purification system.** If you will be collecting water from a stream or lake, you will need to purify it. Everyone should start the trip with a bottle of clean water, but as the trip goes on, you will need to collect and purify water on-site. Chapter 1 provides an in-depth comparison of the methods available, but in short, the boiling option is great when camp is set up. You will need another option on the snowy trail, however, if someone runs dry.
- **Thermometer.** This is excellent for telling just how cold it is.
- **Paperwork.** Be sure to carry all essential paperwork with you on your trek (e.g., medical forms, at-a-glance forms), and leave your travel plans with a responsible party who is not trekking with you. Be clear about your departure and arrival times, and give a buffer—a grace period for checking in at the end to account for delays (see chapters 1 and 2 for essential forms and trip planning).

Personal Gear

As indicated previously, each participant is responsible for their personal gear.

Clothes

The big question many participants ask is "How should I dress?" We demand that everyone wear synthetics and wools on all winter outings. We address this fabric rationale, along with layering technique, in chapter 3. Some winter trekkers like to wear more traditional clothing, preferring natural fibers over synthetics. With enough practice with thermal regulation, duck canvas outer layers can be a viable option.

Every participant should have the clothes in this list plus a backup set that provides a complete change for the base layer and midlayer. (Pack backup layers into a medium-size duffle bag and wrap it in a McGee tarp to add to the base load on the toboggan. The extra hat, mittens, and even a pair of socks can be stowed in a Conover pack.) We try to follow an industry standard for backcountry layering by following the three Ws: wick, warm, and weather (wind and water), as discussed in chapter 3.

- **Bottoms.** Light long underwear (base layer); heavy long underwear (midlayer); heavy wool or synthetic pants, nylon wind pants, or duck canvas pants (outer layer)
- **Tops.** Light synthetic or wool long sleeve shirt (base layer); medium-weight wool sweater (midlayer); heavy-weight wool or fleece sweater (jacket style), windproof shell, or duck canvas anorak (outer layer); parka (with down or synthetic insulation) with a hood (top layer)
- **Extremities.** *Head*—warm wool or fleece hat; wool or fleece scarf, neck gaiter, or balaclava. *Hands*—heavy wool mittens and mittens covers (leather or nylon), or down mittens for those susceptible to really cold hands. *Feet*—heavy wool socks (four or five pairs) or synthetic base socks covered with medium-weight wool socks; waterproof winter footwear (e.g., Sorel or Kodiak) and replacement felt boot liners.

Sleep Kit

Getting a good night's sleep is key—rest is essential on a winter trek. Although the suggestions here can contribute to a good sleep, there is nothing you can do about a snoring tent mate. (If you have not read the poem "The Cremation of Sam McGee," now might be a good time.)

A night owl in the tent can be the stove watcher, or people can take turns maintaining the fire throughout the night. If the tent becomes too warm, people can unzip their sleeping bags halfway. I like to let the stove go out for a cooler, more comfortable sleep.

In addition to the following, other items to have in the tent are camp slippers (slip-on booties for roaming around inside the tent), an LED headlamp with extra batteries, a candle lantern with extra candles, and cards or other tent games to pass the long hours before sleep. All of the following items should be packed into one small duffel bag (with the exception of large sleeping pads, which can be folded under the duffle bags and packed on the sled).

• **Sleepwear.** Cotton shorts, lightweight lounging pants, and a T-shirt (it can get warm in the tent) can serve as sleepwear.

• **Sleeping bags.** Winter sleeping bags (down or synthetic) should be rated from –12 to –20 degrees Celsius; this rating can be achieved by layering two three-season bags.

• **Sleeping pads.** A sleeping pad should be a thick, closed-cell foam or self-inflating pad; I recommend doubling up by using both, or two closed-cell foam pads. Remember, the ground is a block of ice—the more you are insulated from the cold, the better you will sleep.

Toiletries

Pack a toothbrush, toothpaste, floss, lip balm, vitamins, a small wash cloth, a towel, and toilet paper into a medium-size or small duffle bag. Wrap the toiletries bag in a McGee tarp and add it to the base load on the toboggan. (Another supply of toilet paper can be with the trekking gear in the Conover pack for access while on the trail.)

Trekking Gear

Everyone on a trek should carry a thermos (mug style); two 1-liter water bottles; a wide-mouthed bottle for carrying gorp or trail mix (500 to 750 ml, or 17 to 25 oz) (shaking into your mouth is much easier and more comfortable than pulling off mittens and digging into a plastic bag); sunglasses and sunscreen; a whistle; and snowshoes, of course (see chapter 6 for sizing and styles). Backcountry ski or hiking poles can be helpful in deep snow or hauling gear up hills. Other items are ski goggles, binoculars, a camera (batteries and cold don't mix well—know your equipment), rain gear (jacket and pants), small first aid kit (for minor cuts, blisters, sunburns), personal medications, and toilet paper. Trekking gear can be stowed in a Conover pack, along with extra socks and other items to ensure comfort on the trail.

Packing a Toboggan

The next big question we get from participants is "How does all this [i.e., McGee tarps, duffle bags, Conover pack, kitchen box] pack onto a toboggan?" Before every trip, we bring a couple of toboggans—one for participants and one for group gear—into an inside space for a warm practice packing session. Loading a toboggan takes practice, and cold hands affect the learning curve. All participants bring their duffle bags and have a practice run in packing and loading. This also gives us a chance to do a personal gear check to make sure everyone is trip ready.

We warn you now: Packing in the cold with bare hands is not fun. We recommend buying lightweight synthetic weave gloves (they often come in packages of three to five in hardware stores); they provide a degree of protection but do not impede the feel required for weaving in the lashing straps.

Here are the steps for loading toboggans:

1. Make sure the lashing lines (webbing) are free of the fixed anchors attached to each wooden crosspiece.

2. Lay the McGee tarp over the toboggan, making sure that the triangular end is past the curved hood and past the back end (lift and look).

3. Lay out sleeping pads, groundsheets, duffle bags, and assorted group gear (according to which toboggan you are loading); begin to wrap the load with the tarp, and make sure to bring in the triangular ends as part of the fold.

4. Take the lashing straps and cross over the wrapped load. Feed each strap into a running line on one side; then cross over and feed it into the anchor on the other side. Continue this process until the entire load is secure and the end of the lashing strapped is tied off.

5. Issue each toboggan (group of three participants) a couple of Conover packs (they come in small, medium, and large—you can usually find combinations to fit the toboggan length). Think of the Conover pack as a day pack for the extras and essentials. Participants can fill their Conover packs with snack items, extra mittens and a hat, a fleece, a camera, a saw, a first aid kit, an ice scraper—anything they might need quick access to during travel, so you don't have to unwrap the base load. Place the Conover packs on top of the base load, and secure them with additional straps to the anchor points where the lashing line went through.

Thermoregulation: Dressing for Winter Hauling

Avoid overheating, which will cause you to sweat and saturate your layers with moisture. Fabrics that breathe, allowing moisture to escape, are crucial. I prefer an outer anorak made of duck canvas to block the wind; mine is large and bulky to accommodate layers underneath and to trap air being warmed by my body.

Always carry a complete replica of your day clothing. What you wear while traveling and hauling can be dried that night in camp, but you need a second set to wear until the fire gets going.

A duck canvas outer shell breathes, but traps body heat—this one is large to provide room for wool layers underneath. When I am hauling, I remove this and my heavy wool hoodie layer and stow them in my Conover pack.
© Andrew Foran

Leader Tips

Before you lead others on extended winter excursions, we recommend that you gain expedition experience by taking courses or spending time with seasoned outdoor guides. In addition to more formal learning, commit to remaining open to others' ideas, reflecting on best practices, and being willing to challenge your own leadership capacity. Following are some tips and essential skill sets for leading winter expeditions:

• Before you start hauling, when everyone is at peak energy, remind the group about taking turns; everyone should have a turn hauling the toboggan. Those who are not hauling should be ahead breaking trail and establishing the snow gutter, packing the snow for the freight line! On climbs, people not breaking trail can get behind the toboggan to help push the load; that little bit of support can make all the difference. On downhills, those not breaking trail can be at the back end controlling the brake line to prevent the toboggan from running into the heels of the hauler. One last little hauling task is to have someone stand alongside the hauler when starting; this person grabs onto the tumpline and helps get the toboggan started. Having this extra bit of power on a hard start makes a huge difference. Once the hauler has momentum with the toboggan, the assist can call out "All yours."

• Establish a winter buddy system, and conduct periodic group check-ins. Buddies are responsible for looking out for each other regarding extremity sensations (toes and fingers), signs of frostbite on the face (don't forget about fingers and toes), and signs and symptoms of hypothermia. In addition, you should check in with each participant about the issues just listed, as well as hydration status, energy levels, and overall morale.

• Give the group about 500 to 800 meters (1/4 to 1/2 mile) of travel at the start, and then stop and say something like "Wow, who is getting warm on this crisp

A group of winter trekkers heading to McAdams Lake, Cape Breton, Nova Scotia.
© Andrew Foran

winter morn?" By stopping and adjusting your own layers, you model the behavior for your participants, many of whom will follow suit. You can all stow your shed layers in Conover packs for easy access later when you are chilling on a rest stop.

• Avoid get-there-itis by pacing the group and taking breaks. During breaks, make sure the participants are hydrating and snacking to keep their energy up for the next leg of the journey.

• If you are just beginning to lead winter expeditions, avoid ice crossings until you are absolutely sure of the required conditions for crossing ice safely. Exposure to a variety of lakes and ponds at different times in the winter will give you practice observing ice and measuring its thickness (see the discussion of ice safety in chapter 2). If a lake is unavoidable, shore crawl (if safe), and cross only at the narrowest junctures that are not in a flowage area where the ice could be thin.

• Know the trail and area you will be exploring. Build in some environmental lessons and cultural geographic and historic connections. This requires some time (homework) on your end, but it adds to the experience of your participants. Oth-

Home sweet home . . . for a while!
© Andrew Foran

erwise, your trek becomes just a march in the snow. A bit of local lore goes a long way in taking people's minds off the chore of hauling.

Setting Up Camp

Are we there yet? You will likely hear that a lot. After a day of hauling, your group will want a decent campsite. Once there, one of the first tasks is choosing a tent site, preferably one that is sheltered by trees, off the trail, and away from water sources (Leave No Trace principles apply all year long). The tenting group should then begin stomping down an area of snow larger than the tent footprint. This requires more than a single or double pass. It might be a good idea to play snow dancer (see chapter 6)!

Unpacking Toboggans and Gathering Wood

Once the tenting area has been stomped down, leave it to harden while you lead some participants beyond the tenting area with saws in hand to gather wood. Others in the group can unpack the toboggans. Store empty toboggans upright against trees—it makes finding them in the morning a lot easier if it snows through the night. A few people can bring empty toboggans to the wood gatherers.

Now the group focuses its efforts on procuring quality hardwood for the night fire. Take time to teach participants what constitutes good wood to burn. Although not always available, the best wood is standing dead hardwoods that are not punky (i.e., in the beginning stages of rot—soft, spongy, flaky). Punky wood will only result in frustrated efforts to heat the tent and maintain a quality fire. And don't forget that you should have packed a bag of splits to give your tent a head start.

By now you may be wondering how much wood you need for the night for cooking and heating. We recommend at least three standing hardwoods 6 to 10 inches (15 to 25 cm) in diameter and approximately 13 feet (4 m) high, per tent group. Bigger trees will be harder to fell and haul back to camp. As the trees are being felled, some participants can harvest the twigs and branches to serve as kindling to get the fire going and to bring the fire back if it starts to die down.

Now that the group has lugged the wood back to camp on the empty toboggans (don't forget to stand these up), some people can begin unpacking the tent and sorting group gear. Others can begin processing the wood: blocking and splitting (see the discussion in the preceding section Group Gear).

Setting Up the Tent

The next step is to set the tent up. (Of course, if the group is larger, you will have multiple tents to set up.) Lay the tent parts out: poles, tent body, groundsheet, pegs, guy lines, stove. Now it's just a matter of putting it all together. When you are satisfied with the setup, pull out the sod cloth (an extra flap of nylon fabric at the bottom of most tents). Using your shovels, pile snow on top of the sod cloth and up onto the tent wall about 3 inches (7 cm). This helps anchor the tent and seal out winter wind.

Now that the tent is standing, lay out the groundsheet. This requires a bit of effort and patience—it is a big sheet of material. Make sure to keep it away from the woodstove. Leave about a quarter to a third of the front part of the tent exposed, and position the stove on the fabric hearth. The stove chimney stack should be set up, secure in the pole rest, and wired tight. I suggest at least 6 feet of snare wire to wrap the stove pipe to two wooden poles for support. Make sure that the stove is stable and meets the manufacturer's clearance requirements. Participants can now begin unloading their personal gear from the toboggans

Getting Organized

Developing personal and group organizational systems requires practice. The area where the groundsheet has been installed should be a reasonably flat space on which participants can start finding nesting spots. We recommend lining the groundsheet with the McGee tarps to reduce slipping when standing on the groundsheet. The extra layer also separates the gear, primarily sleep kits, from the cold below and the drops of water from the melt that will eventually gather on the groundsheet.

Once the living quarters in the tent are organized with personal gear and participants have carved out their nesting spots, start turning your attention to warming   nt up and beginning the evening meal. The task of drying outerwear and   vill require some coordination and sharing of clothesline space. Once the stove is at full temperature, clothing, boot liners, mitten liners, and other odds and sods will dry quickly.

There are a couple of important things to keep in mind about living together in a hot tent. First, the stove area (the front third of the inside of the tent) is a work area for making more splits, cooking, and cleaning pots. Outdoor footwear should not go past this point. On the groundsheet, lay out all the sleeping pads for sitting and lounging; sleep kits and personal duffle bags (if there is room) should be at the far back. Do not open the kits until you are ready—this helps minimize the clutter and prevents gear squabbles. Extra gear outside can be wrapped in the McGee tarp right outside the tent. Given the possibility of a nighttime snowfall, standing your snowshoes is a good idea. Looking for 14 pairs of snowshoes hidden under a good dumping of snow can become quite the morning activity. Systems and organization are key to efficient winter living.

Cooking

When everyone is settled, it's time to light the woodstove with the bag of splits you brought with you. Line the bottom of the stove with splits and build a fire on top of them. This helps prolong the life of the woodstove by keeping the steel bottom from burning out. (Another option is to transport sand to line the bottom of the stove.) The surge of heat from quality wood gives you a head start in warming and drying not only damp clothing but also the processed wood. After burning up your wood cache, you can then keep the home fire burning with wood from the field. Stack the wood you process alongside the woodstove (not close enough to catch fire!). Reserve a cache of wood from what you processed to travel with your to the next campsite—this provides a heating advantage.

Once the fire box is in full flame, we guarantee that appetites will demand the next priority—supper! This will require unpacking the kitchen box and pulling out the contents, including meal ingredients. Participants will have packed their own supplies: eating utensils, bowls or plates, and mugs. The group gear includes a spatula, a large spoon, a ladle, knives, pots, kettles, a dishcloth, scrubbies, soap, bleach, hand sanitizer, a wash basin, matches, a lighter, fire starters, and beeswax candles for the candle lanterns.

Water

As the stove is coming online, another chore related to cooking is gathering water for cooking and cleaning. By now the water source has been located (stream, brook, pond, or lake), and most likely some shoveling work is required to access the water. Take special care around moving water—especially a river! I prefer streams and brooks, but I still shovel a flat water-level working space so I am not hanging over a snow shelf trying to fill my water jug. Depending on the air temperature, you may have to use an ice chisel to open a water hole. If accessing water from a lake, an ice chisel is essential, along with a shovel for digging down through the snow to reach the ice.

The next task for all participants is to fill their personal water jugs for the remainder of the night and the next day. You will need a lot of purified water to keep the group well hydrated.

A woodstove at full flame.
© Andrew Foran

Like living in a hot tent with others, cooking on a woodstove is also about systems. Here are a few helpful tips:

- Don't be in a hurry. Things will eventually cook, boil, and fry. You need to learn the nuances of your stove—the hot and not-so-hot zones—so you can move some things along and keep other things warm until ready.
- Never leave a stove unattended or step away from a meal that is cooking.
- Use water from your thermos, which is usually still hot, to gives the pasta, rice, or tea water a head start.

Games and Activities to Do in Camp

Once the meal cleanup is complete (dishes washed, gray water strained, food particles in a compost bag, and everything back in the kitchen box) and damp clothes are dry and ready to be pulled from clotheslines and repacked for tomorrow, participants will turn to some form of entertainment or activ-

Back on the winter trail.
© Andrew Foran

ity: cards, mind games, knife and hatchet sharpening, snowshoe repair, swapping out cracked buckles, sewing clothing tears—our point here is to have something ready. This can be the best part of the day—being with peers, sharing conversation during downtime, and reflecting on changes they can make to improve the travel system. Chatting around the woodstove, listening to the winter wind howl through the tree line, and, if the snoring is not over the top, hearing the ice crack and bang in the wee hours of the morning are camp highlights.

The Next Day

According to your group plan, you have either kept the stove going all night with dedicated fire watchers or let the fire go out. Either way, starting the day will take some time. During the evening, as stories are told and fortunes are won or lost in poker, keep a kettle or pot of water on the stove at a boil. Before turning in, have everyone top off thermoses so that you have hot water ready for coffee or tea in the morning. As the breakfast fire is being made or the stove stoked for pancakes and sausages, boil more water for the day ahead on the trail.

The morning brings another set of camp chores. Keep in mind, as you begin, that moving in the snow and cold is slow—rushing people does not make them go faster. Providing a generous time frame is often helpful. However, the group does need to focus and follow a system for breaking camp; otherwise, you will never get out of the woods. Packing up is the reverse of setting up. If you are spending another night out, save a cache of quality wood for the next fire. Begin packing personal gear and taking it out of the tent. Wrap it as soon as you can to prevent snow from getting into the bags. Once the tent is empty, rolling up the ground-sheet and dismantling the stove are the next chores—but don't empty the stove yet! Clear the sod cloth of snow, and begin unpegging the tent. Roll the downed tent, rebag it, and stow it on the group gear toboggan. Now for the tent poles. You may find them frost-locked at the joints. Most aluminum poles are segmented, and moisture will find its way into the joints; as soon as the tent is removed from the frame, cold air instantly freezes the moisture that has made its way into these joints. With the hot coals from the stove, you can heat the poles at the joints to separate the segments—it takes only a second and provides a painless breakdown! All that is left now is to dispose of the ash and coals. Look for a spot out of sight, dig a snow hole, and empty the hot contents, mixing them with snow to douse any sparks with melting snow.

Now that the toboggans are loaded, excess firewood is spread out, and participants are stripped of extra-warm layers and ready to haul, it's time to set out and see what winter adventures are waiting. We find cold morning travel magical: dry, squeaky snow sparkling in the rising sunlight and columns of steam rising from each breath of the snowshoers and haulers, who are heading for the next destination. These beautiful moments of winter living give us an appreciation of our connection to nature. Everyone who is willing should have an opportunity to live so close to a winter landscape with friends, feel a great sense of physical accomplishment, and share a hot tent adventure. Winter teaches us to slow down and reconnect to a different rhythm. We just need to be willing to let go of the so-called modern conveniences of everyday living.

Summary

I have learned to appreciate extended winter trips and with each outing have discovered better ways of setting up camp and traveling snowy roads. One lesson from each of my trips is that in winter things go slow, and there is no sense in rushing. That includes packing, setting up camp, gathering fire wood, and cooking. In a sense, winter has taught me to slow down and enjoy where I am, the people I am with, and the nature discoveries we made during the day.

Winter traveling, and living in a tent for multiple days, has also taught me that winter is a time to explore the wilderness. With proper preparations, we can be very comfortable, even in deep cold. A winter landscape brings a simple beauty that can only be experienced when you hear the crunch of snowshoes on snow and the swish of the toboggan being pulled behind you.

Reference

Conover, G., & Conover, A. (2014). *Snow walker's companion: Winter camping skills for the North*. Wrenshall, MN: Stone Ridge Press.

Index

Note: The italicized *f* and *t* following page numbers refer to figures and tables, respectively.

About the Authors

Andrew Foran, PhD, began his teaching career as a geography teacher and outdoor educator with the Halifax Regional School Board in Nova Scotia. He is an associate professor at St. Francis Xavier University, Faculty of Education, Antigonish, Nova Scotia. The focus of his teacher education practice is service learning, experiential applications in public school programs, and curriculum development in outdoor education at the secondary level. Andrew's research examines teachers and students engaged in experiential courses and instruction outside of school settings. Andrew has

Photo courtesy of Vince Steele

developed numerous teacher education programs, workshops, and courses and has published nationally and internationally. He is leading a certificate program in outdoor education for physical education teachers and a master's in education with a specialization in outdoor education through St. Francis Xavier University. Andrew's collaboration includes teachers in P-12 education, the Nova Scotia Department of Education and Early Childhood Development, provincial school boards, the Student Insurance Program of Nova Scotia, Nova Scotia Teachers' Union, Department of Health and Wellness, and Sport Nova Scotia. In his leisure time, Foran enjoys canoe tripping and paddling, geocaching and navigation, and leading backpacking expeditions.

Kevin Redmond, PhD, has worked as a lecturer in the School of Human Kinetics and Recreation at Memorial University of Newfoundland at Newfoundland and Labrador, Canada, after an extended tenure teaching physical education in the public school system. Kevin has an extensive background in provincial curriculum development and implementation in addition to chairing various national paddling committees that established standards and resources for paddling in Canada. He has written a variety of canoe and kayak guide-

© Thomas Redmond

books, pictorial books such as *Iceberg Alley: A Journal of Nature's Most Awesome Migration*, and educational books including *Quality Lesson Plans for Outdoor Education*, published by Human Kinetics in 2010. As a freelance writer and award-winning photographer, Kevin has published close to 100 articles, more than 1,000 images, and 75 magazine or book covers. In his spare time, Kevin enjoys salmon fishing, skiing, paddling, hiking, and playing golf. Kevin is currently working and exploring north of the 72nd parallel. Kevin can be contacted at kevinredmond8@gmail.com.

© TA Loeffler

TA Loeffler, PhD, professor of outdoor recreation and chair of teaching and learning in the School of Human Kinetics and Recreation at Memorial University of Newfoundland, is also an adventurer, nature advocate, and professional keynote speaker. She has 25 years of expertise leading people through life-changing experiences. TA is the author of *More Than a Mountain: One Woman's Everest* and was one of three coeditors of *Theory and Practice of Experiential Education, Third Edition*. TA's work and adventures have taken her to 42 countries and all seven continents, and she has ascended the highest peak on each of the seven continents. In 2015, TA was named to the Canada's Greatest Explorers 100 Modern-Day Trailblazers list by *Canadian Geographic*. She has shared her message of "Big dreams, big goals" with more than 90,000 youth in the provinces of Newfoundland and Labrador. TA enjoys paddling, rock climbing, mountaineering, skiing, and hiking.

You'll find other outstanding
recreation resources at

www.HumanKinetics.com

In the U.S. call 1.800.747.4457
Australia 08 8372 0999
Canada 1.800.465.7301
Europe . . . . . +44 (0) 113 255 5665
New Zealand 0800 222 062

HUMAN KINETICS
The Information Leader in Physical Activity
P.O. Box 5076 - Champaign, IL 61825-5076